THE KINGDOM OF GOD
IN AMERICA

*the text of this book is printed
on 100% recycled paper*

H. RICHARD NIEBUHR

THE
KINGDOM OF GOD
IN AMERICA

HARPER TORCHBOOKS
Harper & Row, Publishers
New York, Hagerstown, San Francisco, London

TO

Florence, Cynthia and Richard

PREFACE

THE FOLLOWING chapters attempt to interpret the meaning and spirit of American Christianity as a movement which finds its center in the faith in the kingdom of God. The pattern which is discerned in that movement is complex; moreover it can be suggested only vaguely and in outline. Hence it may be of some help to the reader if the writer indicate at this point why he undertook these studies, what problems he sought to solve and what general conclusions he reached.

In a previous study, *The Social Sources of Denominationalism*, I sought to discover the nature of the relation of religion to culture and to throw light on the complexity of American Christianity by examining the influence of social forces on faith and by tracing the sociological pattern of race, class and sectional interests as it manifested itself in the denominations. The account left me dissatisfied at a number of points. Though the sociological approach helped to explain why the religious stream flowed in these particular channels it did not account for the force of the stream itself; while it seemed relevant enough to the institutionalized churches it did not explain the Christian movement which produced these churches; while it accounted for the diversity in American religion it did not explain the unity which our faith possesses despite its variety; while it could deal with the religion which was dependent on culture it left unexplained the faith which is independent, which is aggressive rather than passive, and which molds culture instead of being molded by it. Furthermore, the only answer I was able to give to the problem of Christian disunity was in the form of a new appeal to good will to overcome stubborn social divisions and to incarnate the ideal of Jesus. This appeal seemed, upon critical reflection, to be wholly inadequate.

The pursuit of these and related problems led me to renewed study of American Christianity — although it is only as an amateur, as one who feels the need of testing the abstract ideas of theology and ethics in the laboratory of history, that I am able to pursue such studies. At first it seemed likely that the ideal of a kingdom of God on earth, which has played so great a role in recent religious thought and practice in this country, might offer a clue to the central intention, the common interest and the independent force of American faith. If Professor Kirk could deal with the ethics of Catholicism, despite its great variety, by tracing through early and medieval history the idea of the vision of God, might it not be possible to use the idea of the kingdom on earth in similar fashion for understanding and interpreting American Christianity? Recent European writers, such as Adolf Keller and Heinrich Frick and many of those who participated in the discussions at Stockholm, had seen in this idea the distinctive note in American Christianity and from their vantage point had been able to discern a unity in our religion which was hidden to the internal view. Furthermore, this idea seemed closely related to that " American dream " which James Truslow Adams had used so effectively in interpreting American history. It appeared possible, then, that the expectation of the kingdom of God on earth was the great common element in our faith and that by reference to it one might be able to understand not only the unity beneath the diversity of American religion but also the effect of Christianity on culture. This expectation might be the hard, unyielding core which kept religion from becoming a mere function of culture; which enabled it to recover its initiative, to protest as well as to acquiesce, to construct new orders of life as well as to sanctify established orders; which accounted for its reformist activities, explained its relations to the democratic, antislavery and socialist movements, and its creativity in producing ever new religious groups.

The attempt to analyze American Christianity by means of this idea of the kingdom on earth failed. It was simply impossible to force Puritans, Quakers, and the great leaders and movements of the eighteenth and early nineteenth centuries into the mold of the modern social gospel. In them a *vis a tergo* rather than the attraction of an ideal seemed to be the moving force. They had a profound influence on culture but it was not the influence of direct attack. The result, however, was not wholly negative, for it appeared that although the earlier movements did not seek the kingdom on earth they were nevertheless intimately related to the social faith and that the

latter was not as independent of traditional religion as it
sometimes assumed. What the relationships were and
what unity obtained in the whole process became clearer
to me as I brought the insights of Bergson's great study of
static and dynamic faith, of Barth and many another contemporary thinker to bear upon the subject. In consequence I was led to certain discoveries in the field of
American Christianity which were new to me.

The first of these was that the idea of the kingdom of
God had indeed been the dominant idea in American
Christianity — just as the idea of the vision had been
paramount in medieval faith — but that it had not always
meant the same thing. In the early period of American
life, when foundations were laid on which we have all
had to build, "kingdom of God" meant "sovereignty
of God"; in the creative period of awakening and revival it meant "reign of Christ"; and only in the most
recent period had it come to mean "kingdom on earth."
Yet it became equally apparent that these were not simply
three divergent ideas, but that they were intimately related to one another, and that the idea of the kingdom
of God could not be expressed in terms of one of them
alone. The social gospel with its emphasis on the kingdom on earth was building on the work of previous generations with their different emphases — emphases which
had implied but not expressed the ideas or the faith of
the subsequent movements. Kingdom on earth without
sovereignty of God and reign of Christ was meaningless,
as the last two were incomplete without it and without

each other. If the danger of Puritanism lay in its effort to attain security by means of faith in divine sovereignty alone, and if the danger of Evangelicalism lay in the tendency to make sufficient the reign of Christ within all, the danger of the social gospel was in its idealism and in its tendency to deny the presuppositions on which it was based. Christianity, it appeared, could follow its grand line, avoiding the perils to right and left, if it remembered not only its goal but also its starting point and the middle of its course, the sovereignty of God and the revelation of his rule in Jesus Christ, crucified and risen from the dead.

Such is the theme of *The Kingdom of God in America*. It is a theme which cannot be developed in a single chapter and the scope of the argument appears only as the whole book is taken into account. This may seem to be an effort to present theology in the guise of history, yet the theology has grown out of the history as much as the history has grown out of the theology. As an interpretation it is selective in its choice of materials and in its emphases, yet it is an interpretation which has come out of the study of the materials, not an a priori design into which historical facts have been squeezed.

May I underscore some convictions which this study has fostered in me and which are even stronger than appears in the book? First is the conviction that Christianity, whether in America or anywhere else but particularly in Protestantism and in America, must be understood as a movement rather than as an institution or series of institutions. . It is gospel rather than law, it is more dynamic than static. The genius of Christianity does not appear in its ethical programs any more than in its doctrinal creeds, important as they may be at times; these are abstractions from its life and become fetters when they are not recognized as abstractions. The true church is not an organization but the organic movement of those who have been " called out " and " sent." Institutionalized Christianity as it appears in denominations as well as in state churches, in liberal programs as well as in conservative creeds, is only a halting place between Christian movements. The Franciscan revolution not the Roman Catholic Church, the Reformation not the Protestant churches, the Evangelical revival not the denominations which conserved its fruits — and denied it — show what Christianity is. Since its goal is the infinite and eternal God, only movement or life directed toward the ever transcendent can express its meaning.

A second conviction is closely connected with the first. Christianity as a movement cannot be represented in terms of simple progress in either an otherworldly or a this-worldly direction, nor can it be stated in terms of dualism, which always implies a static view. The relation of God to the world which is infinitely dependent upon him, but which nevertheless seeks to go upon an independent way, to a fallen world which remains the object of his redeeming love, requires of those who seek to be obedient to the divine imperative a dialectical movement. This dialectic is expressed in worship and in work, in the direction toward God and the direction toward the world which is loved in God, in the pilgrimage toward the eternal kingdom and in the desire to make his will real on earth. It is impossible to express the Christianity of the redemption in terms of a one-way movement toward the infinite and eternal God who draws men to himself, for this God so loved the world that he gave his only-begotten Son for the world's salvation. It is equally impossible to express it in terms of love of the creature alone, for the meaning of the creature does not lie in itself but only in God. The life of the church as well as the life of Christian individuals illustrates this dialectical movement, and American Christianity illustrates it as much as any other. The evil habit of men in all times to criticize their predecessors for having seen only half of the truth hides from them their own partiality and incompleteness. Thought and faith remain fragmentary; only the object is one. A truly catholic Christianity does not seek a synthesis in which this dialectic can come to rest — only God can provide synthesis — but does its proper work in its own time with full recognition of the partial character of its interest and with full faith in the whole organic life which makes the partial work significant. The invisibility of the catholic church is due not only to the fact that no one society or nation of Christians can represent the universal but also to the fact that no one time, but only all times together, can set forth the full meaning of the movement toward the eternal and its created image. One of the great needs of present-day institutionalized and divided Christianity, perhaps particularly in America with its denominations, is recovery of faith in the invisible catholic church. The recognition of the dialectic character and of the continuity of the Christian movement is one aid to such a recovery. It helps us to tolerate, understand and love those who express another phase of the Christian movement than our own group expresses; it warns us of our own limitations, yet encourages us to do our own work with all our might and to seek unity not on the level of hazy sentimentalism but of the active intellectual and moral conflict of those who can contend fruitfully because they share a common faith.

A final conviction is that American Christianity and American culture cannot be understood at all save on the basis of faith in a sovereign, living, loving God. Apart from God the whole thing is meaningless and might as well not have been. Apart from God and his forgiveness nationality and even Christianity particularized in a nation become destructive rather than creative. The history of the idea of the kingdom of God leads on to the history of the kingdom of God. Hence my greatest hope is that such a work as this may serve " even as a stepping stone " to the work of some American Augustine who will write a *City of God* that will trace the story of the eternal city in its relations to modern civilization instead of to ancient Rome, or of Jonathan Edwards *redivivus* who will bring down to our own time the *History of the Work of Redemption*.

In substance these chapters were given in the form of lectures in July, 1936, at the tercentenary summer session of the Harvard Divinity School, and again in January, 1937, on the Alden-Tuthill Foundation at the Chicago Theological Seminary. To Dean Sperry and to President Palmer, to their colleagues, especially to Professor A. C. McGiffert, Jr., and to the audiences in Cambridge and Chicago, I am greatly indebted for impetus and encouragement to bring this work to the tentative conclusion here presented and for the graciousness with which they received these verbal gestures in the direction of a truth that lies beyond my powers of thought and expression. I am indebted also to many students who participated in my classes and seminars on " The Ethical Ideal of American Christianity," and to my friend Professor Raymond Morris who read and criticized the manuscript.

H. Richard Niebuhr

New Haven, Connecticut
April 29, 1937

CONTENTS

THE KINGDOM OF GOD
IN AMERICA

INTRODUCTION

ALL ATTEMPTS to interpret the past are indirect attempts to understand the present and its future. Men try to remember the road they have traveled in order that they may gain some knowledge of the direction in which it is leading, for their stories are begun without prevenient knowledge of the end. They are always on their way before they know where they are going and they are impelled to travel by motives other than a sure anticipation of the goal.

What is true of historical interpretations in general is particularly true of attempts, such as the one we are undertaking, which set out frankly to find meaning in the past rather than to describe the details of what happened. They are pilgrims' ventures on the part of those who are interested more in prospect than in retrospect but who, seeing the continuity of present with past, know that without retrospect no real prospect is possible. In this respect Christians of the twentieth century are like the biblical Israelites who needed to remind themselves in every period of crisis of their deliverance from Egypt, of their wanderings in the desert and their ancient covenant with Jehovah, not only that they might have consolation but even more that they might find direction. Whenever they reflected upon the past they gained new insight into

God's guidance of their way, new understanding of the purpose of their existence and new courage for continued progress down the road of ages. The confused events of the past revealed a pattern to scribes and rabbis as well as to prophets and poets, and with that pattern in mind they made their choices in an ever critical present. In somewhat the same spirit we ask today whether there is in the history of American Christianity a pattern which may perform a similar function for us. Perhaps it might not only indicate the meaning of the present situation of Christians in America, but might also illustrate something of the significance of Christianity as a universal faith which must nevertheless take on particular historical and relative character, whether in Italy or in America, whether in the thirteenth or in the twentieth century.

At first sight the presumption that such a pattern exists seems very arbitrary. Christianity in its twenty centuries and many lands is a Protean thing and nowhere does it seem to be more diverse and multifarious than in America. Here it has no central organization; it has not even such an institutional core as an established church provides, accompanied though it be by sectarian organizations. Here there is no common system of doctrine, nor any distinctly American confession of faith which, like the Augsburg Confession in Germany or the Thirty-nine Articles and the Westminster Confession in Great Britain, emerged out of a great critical and formative period in the past to remain a depository of religious insights painfully won by the fathers and a program of spiritual discipline for their children. Here no national liturgy, no Book of Common Prayer, leads generation after generation to pattern its religious thought upon a classic model or to channel its pious emotions in purified forms of expression. Instead of a history of American Christianity we seem to have here only a series of histories — of Congregationalism in New England, of sectarianism in Pennsylvania, of Anglicanism in New York and Virginia, of Presbyterianism and Methodism and of the Baptist movement upon the successive frontiers, of Lutheranism among German and Scandinavian settlers, of Catholicism in Maryland and among nineteenth century emigrants, of Unitarianism and Christian Science in Boston, of Mormonism in Utah, of the Four Square Gospel in Los Angeles and the Apostolic Overcoming Holy Church of God in Alabama. If one must speak of denominations and sects, of organizations here and there, of movements now and then, how can one speak of Christianity in the United States? Is not this religious chaos, like Bertrand Russell's world, all spots and jumps?

The impression of diversity and pluralism is increased by any inquiry into the connection of Christianity with the secular institutions and movements of the New World. The relations of church and state, of gospel and church, of Christian and civil liberty, of the faith and democracy, of Protestantism and capitalism, of Christianity and nationalism, of religion and popular education — and slavery, and reform movements, and imperialism, and internationalism, and pacifism, and socialism —

these all seem to be ambiguous and confused. When has American Christianity taken a consistent and continuous attitude toward one of the institutions or movements of the secular life so that the historian or spectator was able to say, "There typical American Christianity is at work"? Has it not always been on both sides of every question? Clear-cut, unambiguous, Christian answers to the moral questions which agitated the American generations have been so rare that both the critics of the church, who declare its policy to be one of pure opportunism, and the defenders of Christianity, who reply that the church cannot be blamed since they are only churches, seem to be right.

Under these circumstances one answer to the search after a pattern in American Christianity obtrudes itself upon us. It is the answer of many a social historian and it is offered in its extreme and most logical form by the Marxian interpreters. Christianity in America — so the theory runs in general — is, like the faith of any other culture, an epiphenomenon. Religion echoes in mystical and high-flown language the voice of political and economic interests. Faith is part of the defense mechanism of racial, sectional and, above all, economic groups. No pattern is discernible in the history of a religion until this fact is recognized; then it is seen that the underlying sociological or economic pattern has been faithfully reproduced in the dogmas and liturgies of faith, and the apparent pluralism of Christianity can be reduced to a fairly intelligible order. With the political and economic map in our hand we may trace the religious boundaries and find our way among confusing signposts. We understand that when New England divines of the first and third generations preached about grace and divine sovereignty they were but speaking in their curiously allegorical fashion about the political questions with which their audiences were preoccupied. We see that the quarrels about antinomianism and the qualifications for communion, infant baptism, free will and determinism were really exhibitions of the class conflict between an old aristocracy and a rising middle class, or between the latter and the poor, or between frontier and settled community, or between early and late immigrations. Instead, then, of looking to religious history for a pattern which will help us to make choices in the present we must look for it in the economic or the total social history. We must say: The challenge of the present is the preservation of American civilization — that is, the preservation of the customs which have been transmitted and particularly of the system of privileges which power has established in the past; or else it is the accomplishment of that economic and political revolution which has been the " American dream " from the beginning. Whether or not we will meet the challenge with symbols of the faith on our banners is a matter of slight concern, though there are social conservatives who connect their interests with the religious forms and revolutionaries who agree with them that religion is an inalienable part of the established system of habits and laws.

The sociological answer, so briefly indicated, is exceedingly attractive to the searcher after the meaning of ecclesiastical culture. It satisfies the demand for a simple hypothesis and explains many of the facts which otherwise remain obscure. When the rifts which political and economic sectionalism and racial and national division have caused in the churches are noted, when it is seen how religious thought-forms and attitudes reflect the habits of industrial or agricultural workers or of creditors and debtors, when the correspondence of the forms of ecclesiastical organization to the forms of political structure is examined, when the behavior of Christian groups in times of political or economic crisis is studied, then the evidence in favor of the sociological hypothesis begins to carry conviction. It is so clearly the true interpretation of so much that happens in religion that the student is ill at ease in seeking to exempt from its scope any part of faith. Even though the extreme form of the hypothesis, which sees only an economic pattern in human culture, be rejected as an oversimplification, more moderate theories of the social basis of religion must continue to receive serious consideration. Bergson, for instance, like Lévy-Bruhl whom he follows, demands attention when he interprets religion as in large part a defense mechanism whereby society protects itself against the dissolvent power of the intellect, against discouragement and the fear of death, and whereby it sustains its claims upon the individual.[1] Whether the society in question be a national, a sectional, a racial or an economic group its religion does appear to be largely dependent upon its secular interests and designed to protect them.

It does seem to be true that the function which the American churches have performed, by and large, differs little from that which religious institutions of any faith, at any time, have performed for the societies of which they were a part. Like primitive, Confucian, Jewish, Hindu or Mohammedan institutions they have transmitted the popular mores, identifying these more or less speciously with the good counsels of the religious founder and adding otherworldly sanctions to them. Thus they have brought the rising and always somewhat rebellious generations into line with the habits of the past and so helped to preserve the ever precarious balance of social order. They have fortified the morale of individuals and groups by holding up before them in worship a center of reference for their lives and relating their activities to a supremely valuable reality. They have offered consolation and escape when the sacrifices common life demanded of the individual became too hard to bear. Whether in a medical or in a Marxian sense they have given opiate which enabled men to live amid conditions which remained disappointing and difficult despite all revolutions and reorganizations of society and the so-called conquest of nature.

Such faith gave to Pilgrims, Puritans and Quakers the overbelief which enabled them to endure the poverty, despair and peril of life between a savage sea and an ominously unknown continent. Faith enabled pioneers to preserve or to regain their integrity when the social pressure of law and custom was not present to maintain in tolerable unity the centrifugal tendencies in personal life. Through faith emigrants and frontiersmen transmitted to their children some part of that hard-won discipline of the mind and the passions which a raw land, that was all nature with scarcely any culture, could not impress upon the barbarian spirit of youth. Faith in a later time became the defender of the institutions which had been forged in the rude smithy of a new world.

One notes with sympathetic or cynical understanding the stubbornness with which the second generation of Massachusetts Bay Puritans defended their liberties against Andros and Randolph, fortified by the belief that they were a divinely chosen people. One hears with sympathy also the echoing and re-echoing statements that God had sifted a whole people in order that he might choose the best grain for New England and that divine providence had prepared the way for Christian Englishmen by the plague-effected slaughter of pagan Indians. For men who need to meet such ardors and endurances as did the American settlers cannot live by bread alone. When bread is not available they need to feed on faith or else retreat to the fleshpots of their Egypts. When in a later time all the variations on the theme of the chosen people and of the promised land are sounded — particularly in times of crisis — one is tempted again to say that in Christianity Americans found and formed a social faith which nerved them for the task of living, protected their hard-won social unity and justified them in the extension of their conquests. In effect it did not differ from the German belief in race and culture, or the French sense of democratic mission, or the modern Russian gospel of world saviorhood. These all appear to be defenses against the criticisms of the self, against intellectual doubt, against the disillusionments of practiced as well as of suffered cruelty and of victory and defeat, and against the darkness of the surrounding night which envelops all human efforts in futility. What is true of the nation as a whole with its recurrent faith in national destiny, more or less religiously conceived, is then true also of the separate parts, of sections and groups who find and form a faith which enables them to preserve their solidarity and to defend their peculiar institutions.

The kingdom of God in America, so regarded, is the American kingdom of God; it is not the individualization of a universal idea, but the universalization of the particular. It represents not so much the impact of the gospel upon the New World as the use and adaptation of the gospel by the new society for its own purposes.

The obvious pertinence of such a description of the pattern of religious life in the United States makes it very attractive; yet doubt as to its adequacy cannot be quelled. So Bergson finds it impossible to fit the whole of religious development into the pattern of social conservation and defense; for what, on this basis, is to be done with mysticism and all creative, aggressive, dynamic faith? It is difficult if not impossible to fit Amos, Isaiah, Jeremiah,

Jesus, Paul, Francis of Assisi, Martin Luther and many another prophet into a system of faith determined by social factors. There is in religion, or in Christianity at least, a revolutionary and creative strain which does not allow itself to be reduced to this pattern. To be sure, one cannot deny the presence of so-called secular interests even in the revolutionary leaders and movements; yet faith does seem to take the initiative in these cases. The poverty of the various attempts which have been made to interpret the prophets and Jesus in sociological and socialistic terms is an indication that something very important is lacking in them. They abstract from life to such an extent that the portraits which they paint are unrecognizable. When we turn to the history of American Christianity in particular we are scarcely convinced by the arguments of social historians that a John Cotton, a Roger Williams, a Jonathan Edwards, a Channing and all the other reputed initiators of new movements were primarily representatives of social loyalties.[2] For the kingdom of God to which these men and the movements they initiated were loyal was not simply American culture or political and economic interest exalted and idealized; it was rather a kingdom which was prior to America and to which this nation, in its politics and economics, was required to conform. We may call the strain which they represented the prophetic one, for one distinction between the Hebrew prophets and their opponents, the false prophets, was that the former began with God and his kingdom, requiring the adjustment of Israel to these, while the latter began with Israel and its institutions, which they exalted into a divine kingdom. The prophetic or revolutionary strain demands rebirth rather than conservation; it announces divine judgment rather than divine protection; and it looks forward to God's salvation rather than to human victory. It has been present in American history to an uncommon degree and any interpretation which minimizes it or seeks to explain it in terms foreign to itself is inadequate. It may be conceded that the prophets were closer to nomadic civilization than were their urban opponents, that Paul as a Hellenistic Jew had a smaller stake in the conservation of Jewish culture than had the Judaizers he fought, that the middle class Puritans were in economic revolt against the feudal aristocracy, that there was an alliance between dynamic faith and frontier mentality in the United States; but if we do not presume to reinterpret everything these men and movements have said about themselves or to pretend to a profounder knowledge of their aims and motives than they possessed, we shall find it extremely difficult to squeeze these phenomena into the forms of a purely sociological interpretation.

There is a vast difference, as Bergson has pointed out, between a religious institution or static religion and a religious movement or dynamic faith. The one is conservative, the other progressive; the one is more or less passive, yielding to the influence of dynamic elements in other areas of life, the other is aggressive, influencing rather than being influenced; the one looks to the past, the other to the future. The analysis of religious life which makes only the institution its object and leaves the movement out of account remains very partial and, moreover, cannot do full justice to the institution since this developed out of the movement. Because the sociological interpretation deals with static or passive rather than with dynamic Christianity in America it is unsatisfactory as a complete explanation.

We are put on our guard against this interpretation, furthermore, by the reflection that the instrumental value of faith for society is dependent upon faith's conviction that it has more than instrumental value. Faith could not defend men if it believed that defense was its meaning. The godliness which is profitable to all things becomes unprofitable when profit rather than God comes to be its interest. This ancient dilemma is not solved by any doctrine of necessary fictions but only by the recognition that objectivism rather than pragmatism is the first law of knowledge. Hence if we are to understand American Christianity we need to take our stand within the movement so that its objects may come into view. If we adopt a point of view outside it we shall never see what it has seen but only the incidental results of its vision, which we shall then seek to explain as due to some strange transmutation of political and economic interest.

Every movement, like every person, needs to be understood before it can be criticized. And no movement can be understood until its presuppositions, the fundamental faith upon which it rests, have been at least provisionally adopted. The presuppositions may not be our own; we may find good reason for rejecting them in favor of others; but we cannot understand without occupying a standpoint, and there is no greater barrier to understanding than the assumption that the standpoint which we happen to occupy is a universal one, while that of the object of our criticism is relative. The political and economic interpreters assume that because political and economic interests are primary for them and in the modern world, they were always primary, that because economic value or political power are their supreme values therefore they were always supreme. They can say with Parrington that " the historian need not wander far in search of the origin of the theocratic principle; it is to be found in the self-interest of the lay and clerical leaders "; [3] but thereby they illuminate their own presuppositions rather than those of the men about whom they are writing.

Such an assumption of the relative standpoint or dogma of our own time or society as an absolute starting place is a begging of the question. We make an arbitrary choice when we substitute the dogma of economic determinism or of human self-determinism for the dogma of divine determinism. Moreover it is a choice which bars us from understanding the thought of the divine determinists and which denies from the beginning the validity of their interpretation of themselves and their world. This-worldliness may seem more objective than other-worldliness to those who have never faced their own presuppositions. When they do face them they become aware that their ultimate dogma is at least as much a matter of faith as is the dogma of the otherworldly man. There is, to say the least, no less of pure assumption in the conviction that human freedom or social condition is the determining force in life than in the dogma that the creative source of existence is the ruler of destiny. There is at least as much of the temporal and passing experience of the nineteenth century in the belief that economic classes are the fundamental social groups as there is of the transient experience of the sixteenth in the thought that religious creeds mark the essential boundaries between societies.

Such considerations urge upon us the desirability of seeking to understand the relation of American Christianity to American culture by making the former rather than the latter our starting point. After we have done this we may compare the results with those yielded by the opposite approach and try to understand the relation between religion and culture more adequately than we can by viewing the scene from a single point of view. But first of all we need to interpret our Christianity out of itself; we need to seek the pattern within it, not to superimpose some other pattern upon it. The ideal needs to be looked for in the real, not imported from without. Is there in this multifarious appearance, we ask, a principle of unity? Is there a law of development in this movement? Is there a guiding idea which unfolds itself and which, without Hegelian presuppositions as to its nature and its law, we can understand vaguely at least and in outline?

Of course, every effort to answer these questions is relative to our own situation in this historical process of American faith and can claim for itself no more finality than can belong to that which is itself a part of the moving and shifting scene. Yet the sailor who seeks to find his bearings by consulting the charts his fathers used when they set out on the voyage he is continuing, by noting all the corrections they have made upon them and by looking for the stars which gave them orientation may claim at least that he is trying to be true to the meaning of the voyage.

THE PROBLEM OF CONSTRUCTIVE PROTESTANTISM

I. THE KINGDOM OF GOD IN PROTESTANTISM

ANY ATTEMPT to trace the pattern of the Christian movement in America must begin with the Protestant Reformation. Doubtless Roman Catholicism has made important contributions to American life, and there is also a modicum of truth in the contention that the sources of New World religion must be sought in the sectarian tradition stemming from Wyclif rather than in the Protestant movement led by Luther and Calvin; [1] yet both history and the religious census support the statement that Protestantism is America's " only national religion and to ignore that fact is to view the country from a false angle." [2]

As a religious movement the Reformation was characterized above all by its fresh insistence on the present sovereignty and initiative of God. These terms are usually associated with Calvin rather than with Luther, while the latter is said to have emphasized the doctrines of justification by faith and of the Word of God. But it seems evident that both of these ideas derive their meaning and power from the presupposition upon which they are based; and that presupposition is the divine initiative. It is God who forgives and saves, not man; it is God who reveals the truth and the life, not human reason. Calvin, to be sure, made this presupposition more explicit than Luther had done and insisted more upon the majestic and dynamic aspects of deity; but in either case the fundamental principle of the new faith was the prophetic idea of the kingdom of God. God is king, and man is utterly dependent upon him; he demands present obedience of men; he saves them by pure grace without any merit or assistance upon their part; he reveals himself to the ignorant and humble while he hides himself before the wise and prudent; fear of him is the beginning of wisdom; he is the Alpha as well as the Omega. Much of this teaching the reformers shared with their Catholic opponents, for they had learned it from Catholic teachers and the common Scriptures. The medieval church also taught that final salvation can come only from God, that without his grace it is impossible to see him, that he is the source as well as the goal of life, the seeker as well as the sought. But Protestantism, like every revitalizing movement in Judaism and Christianity, apprehended these ideas again with a vividness that had been lost. What had been habitually believed became a matter of urgent conviction; what had been taught as ancient and accepted doctrine was realized as vital experience; what had been one truth among others became *the* truth. In this sense the idea of the kingdom of God came to be the distinguishing characteristic of the new movement.

The Protestant apprehension of the absolute primacy of divine reality was not only more vital in degree than it had been in the institutionalized faith of later medievalism, it was also somewhat different in kind. Roman Catholicism tended to think of God as the eternal perfection of goodness, beauty and truth to the vision of which the church led its children. " The last end for man," Thomas Aquinas had said, " is the contemplation of truth, and to this end all other human activities seem to be directed." " The end of ends for an intelligent creature is to see God as he essentially is." [3] Professor K. E. Kirk has traced in masterly fashion the history of this Catholic conception of man's greatest good, and has shown how, in pursuit of it, the church carefully picked its way between heresies to the left and to the right.[4] Many passages reminiscent of this view are to be found in the Protestant writers. Certainly the theory is never rejected but always forms an element in the theology of the new movement. Yet it does not appear that Luther, Calvin and their followers were as intensely interested in the thought as were Aquinas and the Catholics in general. It did not represent their approach to the problem of life and God. The divine attribute which impressed their minds was not so much God's changeless perfection as his forceful reality or power. Speaking philosophically, they were nominalists rather than realists. But they must not be described primarily in philosophical terms, for their religious insight was guided by the prophets rather than by Aristotle and Plato. Speaking ethically, they were for-

malists while Catholic ethics was fundamentally teleological; what the latter described in terms of the end
they cherished as a hope while they emphasized obedience to the commandment. But they were not ethicists
in the first place. Religious rather than metaphysical or
ethical terminology must be used to describe them, and
in Christian language the distinction between the Catholic and the Protestant views may be summarized in the
contrast between *visio dei* and *regnum dei*.

To regard the vision of God as the ultimate principle
of the Christian life is to follow in the train of Plato,
Aristotle and Plotinus, however much companionship
with Hebrew seers may modify the Greek outlook on
reality; to say " kingdom of God " is to take one's stand
with Isaiah, Jeremiah and Jesus of Nazareth, however
much Hellenic wisdom may enrich insight and guide practice. To call the vision man's greatest good is to make
contemplation, however prepared for by activity and
however issuing in action, the final end of life; to put
the sovereignty of God in the first place is to make obedient activity superior to contemplation, however much of
theoria is necessary to action. The principle of vision suggests that the perfection of the object seen is loved above
all else; the principle of the kingdom indicates that the
reality and power of the being commanding obedience
are primarily regarded. The first term may also be interpreted to mean that the initiative lies with the one
who seeks to see while the object is conceived as somehow at rest; and indeed Roman Catholicism has always

been inclined toward a Christian or " otherworldly humanism " [5] which believes that man's rational sight is almost, though never quite, sufficient to pierce through to the divine truth. The term " kingdom of God " puts all the emphasis on the divine initiative. The distinction must not be pressed so as to obscure the fundamental agreement between the Christianity of the vision and that of the kingdom. Whether we say *visio dei* or *regnum dei*, " God's first," in Thomas More's phrase. Whether end or beginning be stressed, God remains both end and beginning; whether Christ be called revealer or Lord, he is the mediator; whether one be Greek or Jew, in Christ he is a new creature. Yet it remains true that the differences between the two types of Christianity have been important in the past and are likely to be so in the future, though in no other way than as complementary views of a reality which refuses to be imprisoned even in the forms of a reason that has been enlightened by revelation.

In describing the Protestant interest in the kingdom of God it is more important to regard the content of the idea than its form. Medieval Catholicism also used the concept of the divine rulership of God, but it thought of that rule as an articulated and hierarchical structure while Protestantism represented it as immediate and direct. According to the medieval theory, God had ordered all creatures into a harmonious organism in which the higher governed the lower and in which the church, as the representative of Christ and the agency of grace, was the last mundane governor of men. God's government was manifest in the beginnings and the endings, in the creation, in the incarnation, in the founding of the church, in the last judgment, in beatitude; but the intermediate stages of life were ruled by those who participated in his wisdom, according to the degree of their participation.   Catholicism stood then as now for the planned society of which Plato's *Republic* was the great example. God had made the plan; reason discerned it in part, and revelation disclosed what was impervious to reason.   God executes the plan also, yet he does so by means of mundane lieutenants.   So Thomas Aquinas, rejecting the opinion that God governed all things immediately, had said, " As to the design of government, God governs all things immediately; whereas in its execution, he governs some things by means of others."   Though " God has the design of the government of all things, even of the very least," yet for the sake of goodness in the creatures he " so governs things that he makes some of them to be the causes of others in government." [6]   How this architectonic or perhaps organic view of life was used to justify the feudal and hierarchical order is well known. Under the circumstances the term " kingdom of God " easily came to mean " church-governed society."

To this conception of the divine kingdom Protestantism objected.   Was not the plan which reason discerned in things suspiciously like the plan which human self-interest would have devised?   Why was it that philosophers when they sought to think the thoughts of God after him found themselves thinking about a world in which philosophers were kings and in which the noblest kind of life was one of philosophical contemplation? Why did the reason of monks, priests and popes discover a divine plan which justified their claims to rulership and moral superiority over their fellow men? The identification of the rule of God with the rule of reason and of the latter with the rule of the church were both open to suspicion. The Protestant was no antirationalist; however hard the judgments which he passed on reason he also knew that "the manifold agility of the soul" was one of "the proofs of the divinity in man." [7] But he was almost as aware as are modern psychologists of man's penchant for rationalization based not upon impartial truth but upon self-interest. Therefore he spoke of reason as corrupt and prone to error and saw that the plans which it devised or defended for a divine government of the world were often inventions of the "carnal mind" rather than discoveries of immortal truth. This was the negative part of the Protestant's approach to the problem of the kingdom of God. It meant that no human plan or organization could be identified with the universal kingdom since every such plan was product of a relative, self-interested and therefore corrupted reason.

The positive counterpart of this negation of all human sovereignty was more important. It was the affirmation of God's direct rule. He governed all things immediately by the word of his mouth, and to him all political organizations, churches and individuals were directly responsible. In place of the hierarchical structure in which the higher governed the lower, the Protestant set forth the idea of multiplicity in which many equals were all related directly, without mediation, to the ultimate ruler. In religious life this conception of the kingdom was expressed in terms of the priesthood of all believers; elsewhere it formed the implicit presupposition both of democracy and of nationalism, though in these areas the principle took a long time to work itself out. In any case, the confession of the sole rulership of God and the declaration of loyalty to his kingdom was an even more important element in the Protestant faith than was the rejection of mundane representatives of the divine rule.

To times which do not believe in God, or do not do so very much, the sincerity with which religious Protestantism maintained this principle will be suspect and the power which it conferred will remain an enigma. They will criticize the Protestant movement as an inconsistent liberalism and will explain that it derived its strength from the forces of self-interest which it unleashed in defiance of its own dogma. But Protestantism was never liberal in the sense that it made the free man the starting point of its theology or its ethics. The human freedom of which it spoke was not a presupposition but a goal; so far as man was concerned it presupposed his bondage to sin. Its real starting point was the free God. So Calvin confessed:

We are not our own; therefore neither our reason nor our will should predominate in our deliberations and actions. We are not our own; therefore let us not presuppose it as our end to seek what may be expedient for us according to the flesh. We are not our own; therefore let us, as far as possible, forget ourselves and all things that are ours. On the contrary, we are God's; to him, therefore, let us live and die. We are God's; therefore let his wisdom and will preside in all our actions. We are God's; towards him, therefore, as our only legitimate end, let every part of our lives be directed.[8]

The statement is characteristically Protestant in its rejection of the liberal assumption that man must begin with himself, with his reason, his will, his ideals, his self-possession. It is even more characteristic in its direct assertion of the divine sovereignty and in the implicit rejection of the claims of any institution or creature to possess men in the name of God.

Besides vividness and absoluteness there was a third element in the Protestant idea of the kingdom — the note of temporal immediacy. A recent interpreter of Francis of Assisi has remarked that his conceptions of the kingdom of God and its coming were formally identical with those taught by the church in his day, but differed from the latter in the way in which they were held. " In him the consciousness of the *reality* and the *nearness* of the coming aeon was alive, and became the most powerful motive of his religious activity." [9]   A similar judgment may be made of the Protestant movement in the sixteenth and seventeenth centuries. Medieval Catholicism with its spiritualized doctrine of the coming kingdom represented the adjustment of Christian faith to the long postponement of Christ's return and redemption of his promise. At best this adjustment was a remarkably successful attempt to hold fast by means of spiritual reinterpretation to the promise of ultimate fulfillment, and to order the present life with respect to the final end.[10]   At worst, it stood for the hallowing of the present world, for the conservative effort to maintain the existing order by referring the unsatisfied demands of the people to the future and by postponing any radical rearrangement of society.   The new movement was impatient not only with the system of mediators of divine rule and grace but also with the deferment of the fulfillment of life's promise. Its word was " now."   Justification was *now* to be apprehended; assurance of salvation was *now* to be received; the rule of Christ was *now* to become effective.

Not only impatient expectation but also the sense of a crisis in time made the coming kingdom seem very real and near.   All around there were signs that the old order of life was passing; an ominous sense of catastrophe and an invigorating promise of newness of life were conveyed by the rumors of battle, of Roman decadence, of new worlds discovered, of novel ideas and inventions.   In the sixteenth century the Anabaptists on the Continent were particularly affected by the idea of the nearness of the kingdom, but the more orthodox wing of the reform movement shared in it also.   In seventeenth century England the radical sects of the civil war and the Commonwealth proclaimed the Fifth Monarchy, but more conservative Puritans were also living in expectation of the coming judgment and restoration.   In all such moments, when old things are passing and the new has not yet appeared, the important element in the expectation of the

end and the new beginning is not the millenarian myth —
the imagery of fire, falling stars and cloud-borne messiahs,
the cryptic numerology — but rather the conviction that
life is a critical affair, that nothing in it is abiding, that
nothing temporal is able to bear the weight of human
faith, and that salvation is possible only through giving up
allegiance to the passing world and setting one's hope
upon the eternal. The sense of crisis fosters a revolutionary temper among those who have no faith in the literal
fulfillment of Oriental prophecies, for it confronts them
with the necessity of facing the ultimate realities in life.
So for Protestants the sense of catastrophe and newness of
life gave urgency to the idea of the kingdom of God; it was
necessary to press into it, for the time was short; the great
revolution which would make all things new was no
longer a dim dream and a mere culmination of ordinary
life, but it was near and it was threat as much as promise.
Once again, as so often before, the announcement which
Jesus had made pierced the hearts. " The kingdom of
God is at hand."

In these three respects the Protestant movement in the
sixteenth and seventeenth centuries found its center, its
motive and its goal in the kingdom of God. But the apprehension of God's primacy, immediacy and nearness
placed it in a great dilemma. How could such a principle
be used for the construction of a new order of life? *

* I am trying to speak throughout these chapters of Protestantism as
a positive affirmation of the Christian gospel rather than as an anti-
Catholic movement. Insofar as it was a dynamic manifestation of the
Christian faith it was in opposition to the static form which faith had

II. The Dilemma of Protestantism

Insofar as Protestantism was a movement of protest its principle of the kingdom of God was very effective. In the name of the kingdom it could challenge the absolute claims of every relative power, particularly the claim of the great colossus which bestrode the medieval world. The institutional church was required to give way to the living word of God, conceived in the beginning in no biblicist but rather in a prophetic sense. In the light of the coming judgment the relativity and temporality of the feudal-hierarchical order were revealed and it was deprived of the halo it had worn. The ecclesiastical mores, with their exaltation of the religious and their practical depreciation of the secular life, with their regulations of private, family, political and economic behavior, with their stabilization and defense of social habits formed under conditions now rapidly vanishing, were deprived of their sacrosanct character. The pall which hung over the world, the sense of the indefinite continuation of present goods and evils among which men needed to prepare themselves for a remote heaven, was lifted. The old habits and institutions which stood in the way of the new forces in social life had been able to offer effective resistance so long as they evidently represented the universal as

---

assumed in the church; insofar as it became static in turn it had little if any advantage over its Catholic rival. We shall look in vain if we seek to find in the Protestant ecclesiastical institutions the characteristic features of the Protestant movement; if they are there at all they appear in a form which denies as much as it represents the original intention.

against the particular, the eternal as against the temporal. Now they were challenged in the name of the very universal and eternal truth which they claimed to represent. Protestantism furnished a revolutionary philosophy to the new forces which were stirring in the political, economic and racial world. What had been mere revolt, a blind striking out against superior power, became revolution, a movement with a principle of its own.

It was probably inevitable that then, as in later similar situations, revolution should express itself in ways which those who had supplied the philosophy could scarcely acknowledge or condone. While they were interested in supplanting the kingdoms of this world with the kingdom of the Lord and his Christ, these other revolters were obviously bent on erecting new kingdoms of men on the ground previously occupied by the Roman Catholic Church. While the religious leaders affirmed the power of God against all human powers, the secular movements identified their own power with the divine. They seemed to believe that since the exercise of absolute power by the papal church was wrong its exercise by the opponents of the papacy was right. If the church had no claim to the supreme political power, did not this mean that kings had the right to claim that power? If the church was in error in maintaining complete rulership over the economic life, did not this show that the economic man was entitled to rule himself? In place of the absolute claims of one relative institution or person other relative institutions and individuals were to be made absolutes. So

Protestantism faced the difficult problem of inducing emancipated persons and societies, nations and governments, to accept a new discipline in place of the old. It was required by these circumstances to move from protest and criticism to construction. The new freedom was not self-organizing but threatened anarchy in every sphere of life.

Difficult as was this problem the peculiar dilemma of Protestantism did not lie here. Every revolutionary movement needs to meet the same problem and in the course of time every such movement — if its leaders have sufficient will to power, an adequate idea of what they want, and the necessary ruthlessness and diplomacy — is usually able to bring some order out of chaos. The dilemma of Protestantism lay rather in these factors: it had no will to power and in view of its positive principle could have none, for supreme power belonged only to God and evil resulted from every human arrogation of his dominion; it had no definite idea of the end toward which it was traveling and could have none, since the future lay with the free God; and it could not be ruthless since it had the inhibiting commandments of the gospel ever before it. As a theory of *divine* construction the Protestant movement was hard put to it to provide principles for human construction. Yet it was unable to be supine, awaiting in patience what God might do, since it was evident that men lived in a crisis and that they could not stand still but were hastening either to destruction or to life. It was necessary to press into the kingdom.

One of the areas in which the dilemma of loyal citizens of the kingdom came to expression was the field of morality. The Protestant saw how relative were the judgments about good and evil, about right and wrong, and how much the moral commandments of society were conditioned by the interests of the powerful. He was convinced, moreover, that true goodness, a righteousness which was self-forgetful and interested in the good for its own sake, came only as a gift of God, since all the efforts of moral men were bound to be efforts to exalt the self in the sphere of morality while the love of good for its own sake could come only through the self-revelation of the good. He believed that God by his free, unfettered grace justified men without "works of the law" and brought forth in them the fruits of a reconciled life. If this was the case what could man do? How was he to organize his life so as to achieve the desired results? Catholicism with its teleological and hierarchical ethics was able to give definite counsel to the individual. It prescribed to him the pattern of a holy life, in which virtues and vices were arranged in a scale and in which the path to perfection was marked out into definite stages. But what ethical construction was possible to a formalism which proclaimed, "Obey God, love God and do what you please"? What definite counsel could be given to the man who sought perfection when perfection was defined not as matter of behavior but as an affair of faith and love, neither of which was subject to man's control? [11] The Protestant principle was a splendid critical device for deflating the pretensions of moralism, for protesting against legalism and for showing that no particular vocation of man brought him nearer to infinite goodness. It released the laity from the inhibitions of a spuriously bad conscience, which had afflicted it with a sense of its inferiority to contemplative monasticism. But it seemed to lack all the qualities necessary for organizing the lay life. There was no precision in it; it offered no standard whereby men could make choices between relative goods and relative evils; it gave them no scale of values whereby their interests could be harmonized and the higher be made to control the lower. The Catholic critic seemed unanswerable when he said that Protestantism led to moral anarchy.

What was true of the moral sphere was perhaps even more true of the political and economic. In the name of divine sovereignty one could protest against the assumptions of absolute authority by bishops and princes; but the same principle required protest against the equally arbitrary sovereignty of the people. It was easy to use the idea of the kingdom as a critical principle for the overthrow of usurpers of God's absolute authority, but very difficult to employ it for the purpose of establishing a new system of political order. While it could be shown that the control of economic life by church and state was an unwarranted presumption based upon the false identification of their rule with God's, it was difficult to supply a new organization of commerce and industry by referring men to the will of God. It seemed inevitable under these circumstances that each emancipated economic man should make himself the absolute, identifying his interests with the interests of God.

Protestantism faced the same dilemma in religion. The great usurpation of the kingdom with which it needed to deal in its time was neither the political usurpation of the seventeenth and eighteenth nor the economic usurpation of the nineteenth and twentieth centuries. It was rather the ecclesiastical one, for the church then claimed the place of rulership which princes and businessmen assumed later on. Protestantism could not fail to draw the conclusion that renunciation of power by the church was the inescapable corollary of its acknowledgment of the sovereignty of God. Whereas others had said, and were to say, that because God is king therefore we — his people, his church, his class — have a right to rule in his name, the gospel required Protestants to say, because God is king we — who are always prone to pride and sin — have no right nor reason to assume rule. The church in particular had even less right to claim absolute authority than had the secular powers, since it was the foundation of Jesus Christ who had emptied himself and made himself of no reputation and taken upon himself the form of a servant, who had said that his disciples were not to follow the political pattern of the gentiles with their lordly kings.

Nevertheless the religious life needed to be organized, and mere reference to the divine Lord Jesus Christ as the ruler of the church seemed to leave the way open to every sort of individual inspiration, to all the wild plans of self-appointed spokesmen for God. It was good to say that the Word of God alone should rule the church, but how was the Word of God to be understood, who was to declare it, when and where and to whom was it to be proclaimed, by whom enforced? Was not the Catholic critic again right in his judgment that Protestantism stated the alternative erroneously when it offered men the choice between the rule of the church and the rule of God? Was not the alternative rather one between an authoritative church and the religious anarchy of wild sectarianism in which every group and every individual could claim to speak for God?

To the degree in which the conviction of God's sovereignty was present Protestantism was unable to escape from its dilemma. Where that conviction was feeble, where a secular interest had merely employed the new theology as a weapon against old established forms, there was little difficulty. There the older idea of the kingdom could be adopted with the change from popes to kings, from councils to parliaments, from canon law to economic law; there one could cry, " The king is dead; long live the king." Because the religious reformation was supported and used by many interests which had no more, and often much less, faith in the actual presence of divine power than their opponents possessed, it has been possible to interpret the whole movement as a nationalist or as a capitalist revolt. But no one who has read something of the religious literature of the Reformation and

who is not committed to the position that faith is epiphe-
nomenal while political and economic interests are always
fundamental, will be able to interpret the movement in
such simple fashion.   The conviction of God's initiative
and activity was very real in it; his justifying grace was experienced by men who cast their cares upon him and who
brought forth fruits of the spirit in repentant, faithful
lives.   Such men were prevented by their convictions
from seizing power in church and state and from regarding themselves as new vicegerents of God. Since God
himself was on earth as well as in heaven such a presumption was impossible.   How unwise it was the recent fall of
Roman power clearly showed, while those versed in the
Bible could read the lesson on many pages of the Old and
New Testaments.   Furthermore, insofar as men were
truly repentant and faithful they needed little government in either church or state.   They did not resist evil
but loved goodness; they counted each the other better
than himself; they had no need of courts, laws, police,
military establishments.[12]   Yet it was apparent that — as
a proverb of the day put it — true Christians live very far
apart, and that even a convinced Christian's repentance
and faith were never complete nor secure.   The church
itself was not wholly made up of genuine citizens of the
kingdom so that love and concord made law and authority in it unnecessary.   God exercised his judgment,
but his care for his rebellious children was too long-suffering for their own and their neighbor's comfort.   The
dilemma of the ancient church appeared again.   How is

it possible to live in a divinely governed world which is yet corrupted? How may one live as a loyal citizen of the universal, divine empire in a rebellious state which, though it assumes independence, is yet under the sovereignty of the heavenly Caesar?

III. CONSTRUCTIVE PROTESTANTISM

The problem of Protestantism as a constructive principle may be defined as the problem of life in the dilemma. It has been relatively easy to escape the problem by making one of the new powers absolute and calling it the kingdom of God; and this solution has appeared fairly frequently in modern history. But the construction was then no longer Protestant; it was monarchical, capitalistic, democratic or socialistic. It has also been easy to escape by way of a skepticism which, denying the absoluteness of all temporal powers, denied the reality of any absolute as well. This method, too, has involved denial of the fundamental Protestant principle of the kingdom. The Protestant movement itself has needed to find its way between these heresies to the right and to the left. Of course, it has not done so without coming frequently and dangerously near to the one or the other. Seeking to escape anarchism in religion it has come exceedingly close to a new absolutism; the reaction against the latter has brought it into close proximity to skepticism. And so the movement has gone on; but insofar as it has been a vital movement the principle of the kingdom of God has rescued it again and again from lapsing into one of the heresies, though never without the loss of some of its adherents.

Since the concern of the present essay is with this dialectic of the kingdom of God in America, there is no need to deal at length with the various efforts made in Europe to turn Protestantism from criticism to construction. Yet brief characterizations of the three main types of constructive Protestantism in Europe are desirable, since the American movement derived much from them.

The constructive Protestantism of Luther staked everything upon the freedom of the Word of God, with what more skeptical men will continue to regard as too great a trust in the power of the Word alone to sway princes, ecclesiastics and the rulers of economic life. The motto of Lutheranism from the beginning was,

> " *Das Wort sie sollen stan,*
> *Und kein Dank dafür haben.*"

German Protestantism has been occupied with the dialectic of the Word and the world, moving through the phase of pure doctrine with its absolutizing of a theory of the Word — to Pietism with its individualization of the Word — to idealism with its rationalization — through liberalism which, freeing itself from the absolute doctrine, relativized the Word as purely historical — to the present phase of an attempted nationalization and the countermovement of a new assertion of the freedom of the Word. This variety of constructive Protestantism is occupied with the sovereignty of God as exercised by his Word over the spirit of man. Luther apparently assumed that God's sovereignty in the realm of so-called "natural things" had not been as seriously impaired as it had been in the realm of spirit, or that actual civil law and institutions truly represented the natural law.[13] Furthermore, he tended to regard all "outward" things with a monastic or pietistic indifference. At all events, his efforts at construction were almost entirely directed toward the goal of giving God the sovereignty over the spiritual life. "What is on earth and belongs to the temporal, mundane kingdom, there to be sure man has received power from God; but what belongs to heaven and to the eternal kingdom, that is subject to the heavenly Lord alone."[14] Only God can rule the spirit of man and only the spirit is really important. Hence the Protestantism which stems from Luther has continued to concentrate its energies upon maintaining the freedom of the Word and has been inclined to yield to political and economic forces in what seem to be purely temporal matters. It has confidence that if the Word is not shackled it will convert rulers and rich men and so produce a paternal, loving, reasonable rule on earth.

The constructive Protestantism of Geneva and Scotland was, as men now say, more realistic. Calvin did not possess the will to power in any marked degree and he was as convinced as any Christian has ever been that the kingdom belongs to God alone, not to any self-appointed vicegerents on earth though they be Protestant preachers.

Yet he was more acutely aware than Luther had been both of the necessity of restraining evil and of the danger which lay in giving human agencies unlimited powers of restraint. He did not regard restraint as a positive step toward the attainment of the good; it was rather a device for keeping the individual and society from rushing to destruction and a protection against new usurpations of the kingdom of God by princes, economic and ecclesiastical leaders. Two further principles characterized this variety of constructive Protestantism. One was its constitutionalism. It is an error to regard Calvinism as hierocratic; the state was no more subordinate to the church in its theory and practice than the church was to the state. They were both subject to a common constitution, the will of God declared in Scripture and nature, and their cooperation was to be assured by their common loyalty to the kingdom which overarched them both. The leaders of the church were doubtless the interpreters of Scripture, but they had no power to compel magistrates to adhere to the interpretation offered. The clear-cut separation of church and state, with both dependent on the kingdom of God, implied an organization of life wholly different from that which the Roman theory of the kingdom of God brought with it. The third mark of constructive Calvinism was universalism. Despite its doctrine of predestination, or because of its acknowledgment that only God predestined his creatures, it resolutely refused to give up any part of human life as beyond hope of redemption. Not economics, nor politics, nor church, nor the physical life could be regarded as merely temporal in significance, as not involved in corruption or beyond need of restoration to the harmony of God's kingdom. Lutheranism shared these ideas in principle but in practice tended to give up the area of " natural things " as beyond the scope of the Word; separatism tried to withdraw from the established social life; but Calvinism insisted with the thoroughness of the Hebrew prophets that God was king over every creature.

It has been thought easy to dismiss the Genevan type of constructive Protestantism with the statement that its principle of restraint led it to re-establish all the attitudes and institutions against which it had protested. It re-placed, we are told, the legalism of the church with the legalism of Scripture, the repression of men by priests with their repression by preachers, the absolutist claims of the papal church with the absolutism of the scriptural institution. There were doubtless tendencies in this di-rection, and if the Lutheran position led to too much liberty the Calvinist principle may be said to have led to too much restraint. But the charge of absolutism is pos-sible only when the care with which Calvinist leaders limited their own claims is forgotten and when the di-alectical process which the Protestant principle made necessary is ignored. Calvinism, like Lutheranism, could not set forth a rationally and completely developed pro-gram for the organization of society and the church. To take some one aspect of the Protestant movement as representative of the whole and to say that the genius of the movement appears in the theocracy of Geneva, as one instance, is to have no regard to the Protestant principle of the kingdom of God. Wesley and Edwards belong to the history of Calvinism equally with John Calvin and John Knox and the divines of Dordrecht.

The third attempt at construction on the basis of the Protestant dilemma was that of separatism in all its varieties. It, too, believed that only God had the right to absolute sovereignty and that man was ultimately responsible to him alone. But noting the stubbornness of the human rebellion against him and the assumption of absolute authority on the part of men, it tended to believe that he had abandoned church and state, dedicating them to destruction. At the same time it was impressed more by the idea of the coming kingdom than were Lutheranism and Calvinism and it was inclined toward literalistic or mystical interpretations of the second coming of Christ. It chose the way of separation from the hopeless corruption of the world, of humble obedience to the counsels of Christ, and with greater or less consistency declined to compromise its loyalty to the kingdom of God by participating in any way in the kingdoms of men. It conceded the necessity of worldly government but refused to share in it. In view of this attitude it was not strange that it produced occasional prophets of violent revolution — men who were more outraged by the corruption of the world than they were devoted to the law of nonresistance — nor that, on the other hand, it brought forth extreme mystics who found the end of their pilgrimage in immediate union with God apart from the world. But neither the revolutionists nor the mystics were representative of separatism. Upon the whole, separatism remained an effort to solve the dilemma of the kingdom by cutting the Gordian knot. The kingdom of God was divided from the kingdom of the world. The former was composed of those who were ruled by the law of Christ; the latter was doomed to destruction. Separatism's main concern was to keep the community of the faithful pure, to work out within it a harmony of love with a minimum of legal control, and to make it sufficient to itself, without dependence on the political and economic life of the non-Christian world.

When the first English settlements were made in North America all these varieties of constructive Protestantism were relatively new. Moreover they were all involved in conflict. Lutheranism in Germany was hard bestead; during the first half of the seventeenth century it was fighting for its life, and for a long time thereafter suffered from the wounds of the conflict. Separatism led an uncertain and hunted existence, a pilgrim's life, assailed on all sides and on all sides misunderstood. Calvinism had fortified itself in Geneva, erecting there a state which had become the pride of many radical Christians and the Mecca of their pilgrimages. It was the Moscow of the time, whose pattern — though none could copy it faithfully — remained the inspiration of loyalists of the kingdom who looked for the time when all the earth would subject itself to the reign of Christ the King.

England, to which the Reformation had come for a second time, faced a century of uncertainty. Nothing was settled and the old order of life was evidently preparing to resist the new. Everywhere in Europe, save perhaps for the Genevan oasis, the new principle was contending with the old and its future was dark. Even when it gained victory it needed to compromise with the old order, which continued to assert itself in the social habits and structures despite overt defeat.

In this situation America became the land of opportunity. Here Protestantism could turn from protest and conflict to construction. It not only could but needed to do so, for while there was no royal or Roman Church here against which to raise protest neither was there any church at all. If there was no Stuart monarchy here to interfere with loyalty to the divine sovereign and his laws, save in the distance, neither was there government of any sort. There were no settled institutions defending the special privileges of the religiously, politically or economically powerful; but by the same token there were no social organizations of any kind to provide for orderly procedure in the contact of men with men.

Whatever else then America came to be, it was also an experiment in constructive Protestantism. Francis Higginson's much quoted statement indicates how conscious the Puritan was of this fact: "We do not go to New England as separatists from the Church of England; though we cannot but separate from the corruptions in it; but we go to practice the positive part of church ref-

ormation, and propagate the gospel in America." [15]
What the Puritan did very consciously other Protestants
may have done somewhat less consciously, for under the
conditions they all needed to turn to the positive part of
church reformation and to solve the dilemma of the kingdom as best they might.   What they did not foresee was
that the positive part of church reformation was not a
structure but a life, a movement, which could never come
to rest again in secure habitations, but needed to go on
and on from camp to camp to its meeting with the ever
coming kingdom.

THE SOVEREIGNTY OF GOD

I. "Thine is the Kingdom"

IT IS A PLATITUDE to say that the hope of the Puritans who came to America was the establishment of theocracy. If "theocracy" be understood in its literal meaning the statement is very true, and it epitomizes all the faith and convictions as well as the fears and perplexities, the experiments and errors, which marked the history of New England Protestantism. But, taken literally, the establishment of theocracy was not the hope of the Puritans only. It was no less the desire of Pilgrims in Plymouth, of Roger Williams and his assorted followers in Rhode Island, of the Quakers in the middle colonies, of German sectarians in Pennsylvania, of the Dutch Reformed in New York, the Scotch-Irish Presbyterians of a later immigration and of many a native movement. All of these had been deeply influenced, if not directly inspired, by the faith of the Protestant renewal with its fresh insistence on the present sovereignty and initiative of God, and all of them faced the dilemma of Protestantism.

The idea of the kingdom of God was dominant in the first period of American development as it is the leading idea today.   Then as now it was the property not of one group but of all the groups which, coming out of a similar past, faced a common problem.   In the early period, however, Protestants did not think of the kingdom in the idealistic and utopian terms which became current later. Our time speaks of God's kingdom when it means an ideal for future human society.   Such a kingdom may be a wish, a plan, a dream, an ideal or a goal.   It is an " ought-to-be," in contrast to the " is."   It is the blueprint of an order of life that does not exist.   There are not wanting interpreters of early American faith who read back into that time this idea of the present.   Parrington writes that " it was to set up a kingdom of God on earth that the Puritan leaders came to America; and the phrase should enlighten us concerning their deeper purpose."   How it should enlighten us he suggests in the same essay when he says: " The more one reads in the literature of early New England the more one feels oneself in the company of men who were led by visions, and fed upon utopian dreams. It was a day and world of idealists." [1]   This is a fairer picture than the usual portrait of the dour Puritan legalist, yet it seems almost as far from being a faithful representation.   Utopianism is also ascribed to the non-Puritan colonists.   How often has not the " holy experiment " of William Penn been described as a venture similar in character to the New Harmonies, the Oneida communities, the Brook farms and Amanas of a later, more romantic day?

Doubtless there is some virtue in this idealistic interpretation of the early American kingdom of God. The Protestants of the seventeenth century lived between two revolutions; they looked back to the revolutionary revelation of God in Christ and they looked forward to his full unveiling, to the ultimate redemption which faith promised them. Yet one who follows Parrington's advice and goes to the pages of Bradford, Robinson, John Cotton, Hooker, Winthrop, William Penn, or to their teachers and predecessors, to Calvin, Ames, Wollebius, Fox, Barclay, Pennington, seeking there the utopian note of nineteenth century romanticism or twentieth century idealism, is likely to be disappointed. When the idealistic note occurs it is a grace note, or it is sounded by some minor player in the orchestra, such as the author of *Wonder Working Providence of Sions Saviour in New England.*

The strain carried by the first violins is realistic rather than idealistic. The leaders do not speak so much of high-flown plans as of grim necessities. It is instructive to pay attention to the reasons which they give for migration to America. Bradford writes that the Pilgrims began " to incline to this conclusion, of remoovall to some other place . . . not out of any newfanglednes, or other such like giddie humor, by which men are often times transported to their great hurt and danger but for sundrie weightie and solid reasons." These reasons he lists as, first, " the hardnes of the place and countrie," i.e., Holland; second, the danger that old age, making their lot too hard to bear, would scatter or destroy the flock; third, the hard labor to which the children were subjected and the temptations to which they were exposed; and "lastly (and which was not least), a great hope and inward zeal they had, of laying some good foundation, or at least to make some way therunto, for the propogating and advancing the gospell of the kingdom of Christ in those remote parts of the world; yea, though they should be but even as stepping stones unto others for the performing of so great a work."[2]   John Winthrop's *Conclusions for the Plantation of New England* exhibits the same strain of sober thoughtfulness with no nearer approach to the utopian idea than is suggested by the hope that the conversion of the Indians may "help on the cominge in of fulnesse of the Gentiles," and by the further possibility that the Lord may have "some great worke in hand whiche he hath revealed to his prophets among us."[3]   In even less enthusiastic fashion John Cotton discovers *God's Promise to his Plantations* not in visions granted to them or in the fulfillment of "an American dream" but in his "designment of a place for his people," by "espieing out" or discovering the land, carrying them along to it, so that they plainly see his providence, making room for them to dwell there.   Among the reasons which warrant removal to such a place there are again "solid and weightie" considerations, such as the "gaining of knowledge," "for merchandize and gaine-sake," "to plant a Colony," escape from burdens and misery, as well as the "liberty of the ordinances" and the flight from corruption and persecution.   To be sure, Cotton entertains a hope, like

Bradford's, that a people rooted in Christ will bring forth fruits of righteousness, but this hope is far removed from the idealistic utopianism of modern kingdoms of God.[4] One wonders whether William Penn, if he had had fore-knowledge of the future, would have allowed the phrase " holy experiment " to slip from his pen. It lies buried amid reflections as sober, practical and contemporary as those of Bradford and Cotton. If these men were not solid burghers, little capitalists who wanted to make the world safe for property, neither were they dreamers who had fed on honeydew and drunk the milk of paradise.

Seventeenth century Protestants could not be utopians or idealists in the popular sense of the words, for they did not share the fundamental presuppositions of uto-pianism — the beliefs that human ills are due to bad in-stitutions, that a fresh start with good institutions will result in a perfect commonwealth, and that human reason is sufficiently wise, or human will sufficiently selfless, to make the erection of a perfect society possible. They were for the most part thoroughly convinced that man-kind had somehow been corrupted; they knew that the order of glory had not yet been established; they were pil-grims all who did not expect to be satisfied in the time of their pilgrimage.

While many writers are ready to concede that this is true of Pilgrims and Puritans they like to ascribe to Roger Williams and the Quakers a more this-worldly attitude. Yet Williams' devotional meditations and letters bear witness to his longing for a nonterrestrial blessedness and to a gentle cynicism with which he observed the working out of human plans, his own included. He wrote:

> Gods children, as travailers on the Land, as Passengers in a ship, must use this world and all comforts of it, with dead and weaned and mortified affections, as if they used them not. . . . O let us therefor beg grace from Heaven, that we may use earthly comforts as a stool or ladder to help us upward to heavenly comforts, profits, pleasures, which are only true, and lasting, even eternall in God himself, when these Heavens, and earth are gone.

As for the coming kingdom, it was darkness rather than light, for " with what horrours and terrours shall these Heavens and Earth passe away." [5] " It must be so in this world's sea," he wrote to Winthrop, " *sicut fluctus fluctum sic luctus luctum sequitur.* And every day hath his sufficiency or fullness of evil to all the children of the first sinful man." [6] Such expressions abound in his letters.

William Penn's expectations of Pennsylvania were high and his disappointment was keen, but not so keen as it would have been had he not known with Barclay that " all Adam's posterity, or mankind . . . is fallen, degenerated and dead, deprived of the sensation or feeling of this inward testimony or seed of God, and is subject unto the power, nature, and seed of the Serpent " [7] — or with Pennington that " man is a captive, his understanding captive, his will captive, all his affections and nature in captivity." [8] Whatever quarrels there might be about the theological definition of human depravity, the conviction of its reality was a common one.

These early American Protestants believed in the kingdom of God, but it was not a society of peace and concord to be established by men of good will; it was rather the living reality of God's present rule, not only in human spirits but also in the world of nature and of human history. His kingdom was not an ideal dependent for its realization on human effort; men and their efforts were dependent upon it; loyalty to it and obedience to its laws were the conditions of their temporal and eternal welfare. "If we would know how the Puritan felt," wrote Peter Bayne — and he might well have added, if we would know how separatists and Quakers felt — "we must resolutely divest our minds of all ideas relating to the divine Being, derived from the habit acquired by men in these last ages of sitting in judgment on the character of God and discussing the quality of scriptural ethics. The Puritans had not risen or sunk to that tender French conception of the Almighty as '*le bon Dieu.*'" [9] Neither had they risen or sunk to the spiritualistic idea of the kind heavenly Father which their descendants often proclaimed as the necessary corollary of the ideal of human brotherhood. They did not begin with an idea of God made up out of the most amiable human characteristics, proceeding then to inquire whether a corresponding being existed; they began rather with that last being which crowns with destruction the life which proceeds from it. This being they had come to trust and to worship because of its self-revelation in Jesus Christ.

The Savoy Declaration, like the Westminster Confession which it largely repeated, is not so much a compendium of theological definitions as a mighty assertion of conviction. Its affirmation of God's sovereignty sounds like a grand *Te Deum:*

There is but one onely living and true God; who is infinite in Being and Perfection, a most pure Spirit, invisible without body, parts or passions, immutable, immense, incomprehensible, almighty, most wise, most holy, most free, most absolute, working all things according to the Counsel of his own immutable and most righteous Will, for his own Glory, most loving, gracious, merciful, long-suffering, abundant in goodness and truth, forgiving iniquity, transgression and sin, the rewarder of them that diligently seek him; and withal most just and terrible in his Judgment, hating all sin, and who will by no means clear the guilty. . . . He is the alone Fountain of all Being; of whom, through whom and to whom are all things; and hath most Soveraign dominion over them, to do by them, for them and upon them, whatsoever himself pleaseth. . . . To him is due from Angels and men, and every other Creature, whatsoever Worship, Service or Obedience, as Creatures they owe unto the Creator, and whatever he is further pleased to require of them.[10]

If we want to know what the Puritan meant by the kingdom of God we must study that considered statement of his faith or, turning to his English cousin, let a Baxter tell us that "the World is a Kingdom whereof God is the King . . . an absolute Monarchy . . . by the title of Creation. . . . God is the end as well as the beginning of the divine monarchy of the world" and "all men as men are the subjects of God's kingdom, as to Obligations and Duty, and God will not ask the consent of any man to be so obliged." [11]   In the refrain of Hooker's *Survey of the Summe of Church Discipline* and of Cotton's *Abstract of the Laws of New England* the faith is summarized: " The Lord is our King; The Lord is our Lawgiver; He will save us."

Quakers and separatists did not differ from other English Protestants in their confession of the rule of God. Their more mystical approach led them to think of him as first of all the Lord of conscience and the inner life, yet they presupposed his dominion over all things.   " If you build upon anything," Howgill wrote, " or have confidence in anything which stands in time and is on this side eternity and the Being of beings, your foundation will be swept away, and night will come upon you, and all your gathered-in things and taken-on and imitated will all fail you." [12]   George Fox's *Journal*, like Augustine's *Confessions*, is a great affirmation of faith in the kingdom of God.   " Blessed forever be the name of the Lord, and everlastingly honored, and over all exalted and magnified be the arm of his glorious power, by which he hath wrought gloriously; let the honor and praise of all his works be ascribed to him alone." [13]

No more orthodox believer confessed the living, sovereign power of God more clearly than did Isaac Pennington:

The Lord God of heaven and earth, of glory, of majesty, of everlasting power, victory and dominion over all, who made both heaven and earth, and hath the command of all things therein, he disposeth of nations, of governments, of earthly powers according to his pleasure, and who may say unto him, what dost thou? Who may implead him for making a rich nation poor, a strong nation weak, or for bringing down the high and mighty, the strong, stout, honorable and noble in a nation, and exalting the poor, the mean, the persecuted? And if he turn his hand again and lay them flat whom he had lifted up, who can withstand him, or who can contradict him? . . . The Lord God taketh not pleasure in overturning of nations, or in breaking in pieces the power thereof: yet if they will by no means hearken, but harden their hearts, and stand in the way of his counsel and design, he cannot spare them. . . . Therefore stand not in battle against him, but bow before him, ye great ones of the earth! [14]

How contemporaneous this kingdom of God was in the Quaker's conception, and how relevant to political affairs, his admonitions to Parliament, to Oliver Cromwell and to sundry magistrates adequately show.

Roger Williams was less deeply affected by the sense of God's dynamic character, more drawn to the vision of divine beauty, yet it is apparent that back of his protests against the compromises of Massachusetts Bay Puritans stood his firm conviction of the sovereignty of God and of the ineluctability of his rule. Persecution is contrary to that rule and will bring destruction. " Oh! how likely is the jealous Jehovah, the consuming fire, to end these present slaughters of the holy witnesses in a greater slaughter! " [15] Doubtless these men all prayed, " Thy kingdom come, thy will be done on earth as it is in heaven," but with even greater fervor they confessed, "Thine is the kingdom and the power and the glory forever and ever."

If the kingdom of God was not utopia neither was it

administration by means of special miracles of the sort in which the authors of *Wonder-Working Providences* and *Magnalia Christi Americana* took especial delight. The God of Protestant faith was not the First Cause of a later Deism, but neither was he the meddling deity of eighteenth century supernaturalism. His relation to nature was intimate and close. Nature, as a recent writer has put it, was like a glove upon his hand. Nothing happened which was not in relation to him and was not therefore a meet occasion for penitence or praise. Yet he appeared in ordinary rather than in special events. His rule was manifested, as it had been for Jesus, in the rain which fell on just and unjust, in the sun which shone on evil and good, in storms by sea and drought by land, rather than in the miraculous happenings which sanctimonious piety, adulterated with superstition, loved to relate and embellish. The Protestants saw the law of God in the immutable ways, in the actual pattern of reality to which revelation had given the key and which reason, following upon revelation, could discern. The will of God was not unnatural in the sense that it was imposed upon a stubborn and refractory nature from without by spirit warring against flesh; it might be called supernatural, if that term implies the presence of power and purpose behind or beyond as well as within natural events. The early Protestant idea of the sovereignty was at least as closely akin to Sir Isaac Newton's conceptions of nature as it was to those of miracle-bound supernaturalists. Yet to interpret it by sole reference to either one of the set of ideas which developed from it in the later, mechanically minded time is to misunderstand it thoroughly.

This kingdom of God was not something to be built or to be established nor something that came into the world from without; it was rather the rule which, having been established from eternity, needed to be obeyed despite the rebellion against it which flourished in the world. It may be likened to the rule of a universal Caesar against whom ignorant tribes had made vain rebellion, deluding themselves with the belief that his power was remote or that it was inimical to them. The Puritans, Pilgrims, Quakers, with their associates, were first of all loyalists. They were loyal, in Chesterton's phrase, to the " flag of the world "; they were convinced that this flag represented power and law as well as benevolence in which men could trust when they had lost confidence in their own good will and in that of their ecclesiastical and political overlords. To think of them as primarily protesters and rebels is to regard them from a point of view foreign to their own. The first thing in their minds was positive. They were nonconformists, dissenters, protesters, independents, only because they desired to be loyal to the government of God, and in that positive allegiance they were united, however much their unity was obscured for later times by their party quarrels.

We shall do well, therefore, when we look upon them, whether in England or America, to heed Carlyle's warning:

By no means to credit the widespread report that these seven-teenth century Puritans were superstitious, crackbrained persons, given up to enthusiasm, the most part of them, . . . the minor part being cunning men who knew how to assume the dialect of the others and thereby as skillful " Machiavels " to dupe them. . . . This is a widespread report but an untrue one. . . . He will be wise to believe these Puritans do mean what they say, and to try unimpeded to discover what it is; gradually a very stupen-dous phenomenon may rise on his astonished eye, a practical world based on a belief in God.[16]

The practical world based on belief in God seems rather impractical when attention is directed to the con-fusion which appeared in early American efforts at Protes-tant construction. The strife of parties, the divisions and persecutions connected with the founding of the New England and the Quaker colonies were an American parallel to the conflict which marked the constructive efforts of Protestantism in England and on the European continent. There was uncertainty here about the organi-zation of the state, about the structure of the church, about the relations of church and state, and about the ex-tent to which loyalty to the kingdom of God was compati-ble with concern for the temporal and passing order. No such simple principles as those which guided the con-structive work of eighteenth century humanism seem to have been followed by the theocentric architects of the new social life. If we would understand their deeds and sayings we are required, it appears, to refer to private ex-periences, personal prejudices and interests, and to the human penchant for inventing abstract reasons to justify the inconsistencies of conduct. No logical, only a psychological or sociological description of the meaning of divine sovereignty for constructive Protestantism in America seems possible.

But the confusion and strife so apparent upon the surface were borne upon an underlying unity, nor were they really more obvious than similar appearances of conflict in the time of humanistic construction. A logical order in which divine sovereignty was the first principle runs through the disorder, and the conflict was at least as much an affair of reason as of emotion and interest. That the latter played their inevitable role the Protestants were as ready to concede as their critics have been to urge, for they knew the human mind to be darkened; they did not except themselves from that universal rule whereby all men are liars; [17] their lips, they confessed, were " uncircumcised." Nevertheless their reason sought its way amid pitfalls and temptations, looking ever again to its first principle lest it be lost completely. From the fundamental conviction of divine sovereignty it moved on to three further positions which were defended by all parties, though with different means and varying strength. We may designate these three positions as Christian constitutionalism, the independence of the church, and the limitation or relativization of human sovereignty. All three of these ideas have left their impress upon American life, though their significance does not lie in their social results save for a point of view which regards God as having been made for America rather than America for God.

II. The Kingdom and Its Constitution

The principle of Christian constitutionalism is directly corollary to the principle of God's sovereignty. Since God is the source of all power and value, his nature and his will rather than human nature and human desires or ideals need to be consulted in all human actions. Furthermore, if God is really the beginning, his character and intention need to be learned from himself and not prescribed to him by means of ideas of his will gained from human nature. God's revelation of himself, then, can be the only basis for the organization of life under his sovereignty. To live in the kingdom is to live under revelation.

That this revelation was somehow to be found in Scripture all Protestants agreed. Even where no explicit statement of the doctrine was made or where the testimony of the Spirit was preferred to the written word, the constant appeal to the Bible showed how implicit was its authority. If it was argued, as by Quakers, that the " inner testimony of the Spirit is that alone by which the true knowledge of God hath been, is, and can be only revealed," and that the Scriptures are a " secondary rule," yet it was thought important to say that this doctrine was " according to Scriptures." [18] If the appeal was made to reason, as by Chillingworth, yet the Scriptures were called upon to validate this appeal, for the Bible was the " only religion of Protestants." Among the Puritans, however, the principle of biblical authority was highly explicit. They tended to give first place to this doctrine in their creeds and fought for it with a stubbornness that often betrayed them into adopting narrow and indefensible positions. The issue had appeared clearly to Richard Hooker who had defined it as the chief source of contention between the reforming and the conservative parties in the Church of England. "Whereas God hath left sundry kinds of law unto man," he wrote, "and by all those laws the actions of men are in some sort directed, they hold that only one law, the Scripture, must be the rule to direct in all things, even so far as the ' taking up of a rush or a straw.' . . . They restrain the manifold ways which wisdom hath to teach men by, unto one only way of teaching which is by Scripture." [19]

To contemporaries and to later critics this Protestant emphasis on Scriptures seemed to be a worship of the letter, but what was at stake for the Puritan was the principle of the kingdom of God, for to give to the " manifold ways which wisdom hath to teach men " a place equal to the Scriptures was to erect the sovereignty of men alongside the sovereignty of God and to make not one beginning, with God, but two, with God and man. He did not despise learning or reason [20] but he was determined to " lay Christ in the bottome, as the only foundation of all sound knowledge and learning." [21]   It was not love of antiquity nor the reflection that the Bible was a good instrument for the securing of human liberties, but his logical consistency which bade him make revelation the foundation of his constructive activities.

Yet the Protestant discovered as he began and continued his effort to organize life under the kingdom of God that the principle of revelation was no simple principle. The equation of the Scriptures with the revealed will of God led to virtual denial of the living reality of God. Men like John Eliot could believe that " we should derogate from the sufficiency and perfection of the Scripture " if we doubted that it contained " a forme of civil Government instituted by God himself." Hence they might try to fashion state and church after the model of ancient Israelites and the company of heavenly hosts.[22] Three things, however, prevented the acceptance of the Scriptures as the whole embodiment of the divine will. The first was the Bible itself. Though it remained for the nineteenth century to discover how completely it was a book of life and movement and history, the seventeenth century was not in real doubt about the essential fact, since it needed to deal with two covenants, with both law and prophets, with both Gospels and Epistles. Moreover, the Scriptures taught the immediate activity of God through his Holy Spirit and criticized severely the worship of the letter. The second obstacle to the use of the Bible as a lawbook was the difference in condition between early Israelites or first century Christians on the one hand, and seventeenth century Americans on the other. Though Roger Williams was particularly aware

of this difficulty the more orthodox could not escape it.[23]
In the third place the equation of the Bible with revelation tended to turn into a denial of the fundamental conviction upon which the faith in revelation rested — the
belief in the living divine initiative — for it could be interpreted to mean that God had virtually retired from the
world since declaring himself to the ancients. With these
difficulties the Massachusetts Bay Puritans wrestled, not
only in the strife with Antinomians, Williams and the
Quakers, but in their actual work of construction, as they
sought to frame laws for the commonwealth and to carry
on their administration. Yet with a stubbornness which
indicated how much was at stake they sought to remain
close to the Scriptures in all their work. And in the upshot their inner as well as their external conflict led them
to the practice of a biblical constitutionalism in which the
revelation of God recorded in the Scriptures was conceived as a double covenant which was not indeed the
source of the laws that needed to be enacted for the common life or even wholly of the doctrines which were to
be taught in the churches, but which was the constant
check upon the vagrant desires of individuals or masses
and upon the subjective inspirations of self-appointed
prophets or the specious reasonings of self-confident wise
men. The temptation of Puritanism was to fall into a
narrow constructionism, to use its constitution not only
as the criterion by which all new ideas and measures were
to be tested but as the source of all such ideas and measures. Nevertheless it was forced to follow the dialectic

into which the principle of the sovereignty of the living God led it.[24]

If Puritans emphasized one phase of this dialectic, separatists and Quakers stressed the other. The two poles between which both moved were the objective criterion of God's present will — his self-revelation through Jesus Christ recorded in the Scriptures — and the subjective criterion — the testimony of the Holy Spirit. The Puritan began with the first and needed constantly to move toward the second; the separatist began with the second and needed ever and again to move toward the first. The Puritan tended toward legalism and authoritarianism because of his desire to avoid individualism and to establish himself in a safe position under divine sovereignty; the Quaker and his spiritual kin tended toward subjectivism and individualism by reason of their desire to find similar security. Both alike were required to acknowledge the principle of Christian constitutionalism, the principle namely that the revelation of God in Christ was the test which needed to be applied in every case to the answers which reason or spiritual experience gave to the question, What is the will of the sovereign Lord for men in this present situation? Roger Williams does not seem to have wrestled with the problem. The spirit of Christ within the soul was for him the sufficient guide of reason in its work of arranging order on earth. That the spirit of that Christ could be known only from the Scriptures he may have taken for granted; " that word literal is sweet " to him, he writes, " as it is the field where the mystical word or treas-

ure, Christ Jesus, lies hid." [25]   As for the Quakers, though
they fought against the literalism which they thought
characteristic of Puritanism and exalted the inner light
above the Scriptures, they were in their early days so per-
meated with scriptural ideas and took biblical authority
so much for granted that they failed to note how dependent they were on the principle of historic revelation.
Though they tended to speak of Jesus Christ and of the
inner light as identical, they actually made the spirit of
the incarnate Christ, described in Scriptures, the criterion
by which to judge the inner light.[26]   Professor Rufus Jones
has described, though in reference to a later time, the
dialectic in which the Friends were engaged from the beginning and which expressed itself in their work of construction in America:

> Nobody in the Society of Friends had adequately faced the
> implications and the difficulties involved in the doctrine of the
> inner light, and nobody on the other hand reached any true
> comprehension of the relation of historical revelation to the light
> within the individual soul. . . . For a whole generation the
> society had tacked, like a ship sailing against the wind, in a curi-
> ous zigzag, back and forth from Scripture to inner light and from
> inner light to Scripture.[27]

The " curious zigzag " is descriptive of the whole
course of American Protestantism, not only of the
Quakers and not only in the early period.   And though
one pilgrim ship was on the starboard tack while the
other was on port, they were carried by the same wind,
their compasses pointed to the same north pole as they

sought the common harbor. Adopting the political meta-
phor again in place of the nautical, we may say that a
grand line of scriptural constitutionalism appeared in the
development of constructive Protestantism in America.
In the long run all the groups manifested a loyalty to
the constitution which was second only to their loyalty
to God and inseparable from the latter. The line of constitutionalism was at the same time the line of dynamic
movement, since the constitution was the record of a life
rather than a law and since it was subject to the free activity of the sovereign who ruled in the present as he had
in the past but did not rule the present by the past.

Connections between the Christian constitutionalism
of the constructive Protestants and the political constitutionalism of the seventeenth and eighteenth centuries
were intimate and close. It has been frequently suggested that the former was dependent on the latter. Yet
the basis of the one was the idea of the sovereign people
and of the other the faith in the sovereign God, and this
divergence in source led to dissimilarity and conflict as
well as to association.[28] It is not evident that Christian
constitutionalism owed more to its political cousin than
the latter owed to the former, or that the dynamic of the
popular will led more to life and movement under the
constitution than did the dynamic of the divine will.
Whatever were the interrelations and whatever the debts
which culture owed to religion, the people of the kingdom of God sought despite fatigue and error to follow
their own line of march under the commandment of the

Lord of hosts.   Whatever they may have thought as they began their work, they discovered as they proceeded that life under the rule of God meant directed movement rather than safe dwelling in unchangeable institutions.

III. The Church Under the Sovereignty of God

The second corollary of faith in the sovereignty of God which guided American Protestants in their work of construction was the principle of the independence of the church.   Positively stated, it was the principle of the dependence of the church on God's kingdom.   This rule, like that of revelation, was not simple, for upon the one hand God was a living God whose ever active will did not prescribe institutions so much as it guided life; and upon the other hand his relation to the fallen world required the loyal citizens of his kingdom to take up into their own lives, individually and as a group, that alternation of direction toward him and toward his creation which was at least symbolically represented in the incarnation, ascension and return of the Christ.   Constructive Protestantism in America, despite all its own unwillingness, was required by the God of its faith to substitute a church movement for an ecclesiastical institution and to carry on that movement in dialectical fashion rather than along the line of simple progress toward a definable goal. The complexity of its work was due to these facts more than to the intrusion of political and personal interests, though the latter were doubtless present and served to confuse the builders of the church.   The grand strategy of life under the kingdom of God, which included retreat from the world as well as attack upon it, the building of fortresses as well as great movements of mighty armies, was often hidden from participants as well as from observers who concentrated attention on tactics, lost sight of the minor part they played in a total campaign, or regarded orders of the day as the ever identical instruction from the remote headquarters of heaven. Yet we may gain some intimation of the strategic pattern if we keep firmly in mind the meaning of the fundamental principle, divine sovereignty, for the work of church construction.

In all times the realization of God's reality has led men to make the gathering of the church their first task. It was so in the case of the prophets who, seeing the majesty of the Lord and the infinite dependence of Israel upon him, turned to the nation which he had created, and persuaded it to acknowledge again its ancient covenant and to be faithful to the divine husband. It was so in the days of the Baptist and of Jesus Christ,[29] and of the Franciscan revival of Christian life.[30] For what is the church save the assembly of people before God, or the movement of those who, abandoning all relative and finite goals, turn toward the infinite end of life? It is the *ecclesia* which has been called out of the pluralism and the temporalism of the world to loyalty to the supreme reality and only good, on which the goodness of all finite things depends.

To the extent that faith in sovereignty is real the building of the church must take precedence over every other task, for if all human sovereignties depend on the divine, all labor upon the organization of political and economic and biological communities must be made subordinate to the realization of the church. Despite the differences which prevailed among American Protestants as to the type of relative organization which the actual church was to assume, they were agreed upon this fundamental principle. As divine determinists, they could no more put political construction in the first place than economic determinists can begin with religion. So the Pilgrims of Plymouth were a church before they were a commonwealth and became a commonwealth only in order that they might maintain themselves as a church. The first concern of the Puritans in Massachusetts Bay, Connecticut and New Haven was the church. John Cotton spoke their mind when he wrote to Lord Say and Sele, "It is better that the commonwealth be fashioned to the setting forth of God's house, which is his church, than to accomodate the church to the civil state." [31] Important as was the Puritan discussion of political issues it yielded first place to debate on the problem of church organization. The great questions were, how the invisible church of those truly called out of the world might be made visible, and how the visible church might maintain itself as a pure expression of the divinely established *ecclesia*. Despite the modern tendency to interpret Roger Williams as primarily a political thinker, it seems impossible that one should read his writings without understanding that he also, like Thomas More and many another Christian statesman, was first of all a churchman. He was a seeker, discontent with every institutional religious organization; yet this fact had positive rather than negative significance. In spirit he was the most otherworldly man of all the New Englanders, a Protestant monk. The concentration of the Quakers in the middle colonies upon the primary task of building the church is evident, whether their positive or their negative action be considered. They dealt with the problems of politics and economics as questions of secondary significance, seeking first of all to establish the true church, to call men away from their " will-worship," to gather the " people of God " into societies and there to maintain them in purity with the aid of personal and social discipline. Whatever issues arose among the various groups, it was clear to all of them that under the sovereignty of the living God man's first concern was the building of the church, not as an institution but as the social expression of the movement of life toward its true goal.

The converse of dependence on God is independence of everything less than God. On this principle also the early American Protestants were agreed, despite the differences which were to be found among them. Since the relation of man to God is immediate, or mediated only by Jesus Christ, the pretensions of princes and bishops, of state or churchly institutions, to represent divine sovereignty needed to be rejected, particularly in view of the fact that such rulers of the church tended constantly to use it for the attainment of relative ends. Calvin had recognized the importance of the principle of independence in Geneva where his first interest had been the maintenance of the church's right to determine its own conditions of communion and to discipline its members, always by reference to the will of God.[32]   There was never any question in America, among the groups representing the Protestant movement, of the necessity of such independence.   Though the Puritans were more conservative than Quakers or Baptists, they went further in the direction of independence than did their English cousins, and so marked the first stage of a movement in which Williams and the Quakers took more advanced positions. Even the established churches of Massachusetts Bay and Connecticut were never state churches which yielded any rights to the state in the appointment of officers, the administration of discipline or the setting up of the form of church government.   In this sense the principle of independence was firmly established in American Protestantism from the beginning, and the subsequent development of a free church was made as necessary by the religious movement as it was by the political.

The recognition of divine sovereignty as the first principle in church construction had more important consequences in the limitation which it put upon church membership.   To put the church under the sovereignty meant that only those whom God himself had " called out " of the world were true members of the church.   Hence the problem of the constructive Protestant was that of adjusting the human institution to the divine working and of seeing to it that none were admitted to the institution

who were not " visible " saints — though it was freely recognized on all sides that men's judgments in these matters were subject to error, so that the church organized
by men would always contain some not called by God and
always exclude some called by God.[33]   Again the principle was a common one which separatists and Quakers
only carried further than the Puritans did, and from the
first it gave to American churches the character not indeed of voluntary associations but of sects which valued
holiness more than catholicity.   The catholic church was
an object of faith.   It was not wholly invisible according
to the Puritans since " the whole body of men throughout
the world, professing the faith of the gospel and obedience unto God by Christ according unto it . . . are, and
may be called the visible Catholique Church of Christ "
insofar as they did not deny their profession by errors or
" unholiness of conversation."   Yet so fearful was the
Congregational Puritan of any usurpation of the sovereignty by national, provincial or episcopal institutions
that he hastened to add, " as such it [the visible catholic
church] is not intrusted with the administration of any
ordinances, or have any officers to rule or govern in, or
over the whole body." [34]   The same concern for divine
sovereignty which led him to desire a church of the elect
alone, so far as man could judge election, led him also to
keep the church limited in power.   With this point we
shall deal more fully later on.   At all events, the congregational and associational pattern which Puritans, separatists and Quakers developed was based as much on loyalty

to the principle of divine sovereignty as on biblicism or on political interests. It was a pattern to which even those churches which came from Europe in a later time and which brought with them established customs needed to adjust themselves.

To represent the church idea which follows from divine sovereignty solely in terms of an *ecclesia* called out from the world is historically and theologically impossible. The direction of life toward a God who loved the world, created and redeemed it, requires of his people return to the world. The American churches were involved from the beginning in this fundamental dialectic of Christianity in which all their predecessors had participated. The paradox of Platonism which causes the philosopher to return from the vision of the immortal truth in order that he may be a kingly guide of the people represents this dialectic. It is paralleled also in the Eastern idea of the bodhisattva who absents himself from felicity awhile in order that he may enlighten others. It is crudely and falsely stated in the abstract and static terms of the transcendence and immanence of God and of the requirements these make upon man. It is set forth symbolically and more than symbolically in the story of creation, fall, incarnation, ascension and the coming of the Holy Spirit. Devotion to the same sovereign God who calls his people out of the world requires of them service to and in the world. So Puritans, separatists and Quakers who had fled the corruptions of secularized Christianity needed in turn to flee from the perils of a celestialized or spiritualized faith. In various ways they sought to fulfill the double yet not dualistic purpose of the Christian calling.

The Puritans were most aware of the danger of separatism and tried to remain faithful to both ideas at the same time. Hence they attempted to translate the dialectic movement of the Christian life into a stable, organized synthesis in which church and state represented the two aspects of Christian society, sainthood and citizenship the two directions in personal Christian life. Though separatists and Quakers emphasized the movement away from the world, they were acutely conscious of the Christians' mission. Instead of seeking synthesis they trusted the guidance of the spirit who was life and truth. Actually they were as interested and as effective in bringing Christian principles to bear on government and economics as the Puritans were. Their experiments differed from those of Massachusetts and Connecticut partly as the dynamic differs from the static, but in both cases the same fundamental pattern derived from God's relation to the world was illustrated.[35]

To trace the pattern in its details is impossible within the limits of this study and to do so might not be fruitful. It is sufficient to point out that the engagements in and withdrawals from political life in both New England and Pennsylvania correspond to the dialectical pattern and must be regarded not as illustrations of the failure of Christianity to deal with secular problems but rather as examples of the method which is dictated by the fundamental human situation. No stable institutional organi-

zation once and for all established but only the movement
Godward and in God's name worldward can express the
faith in the sovereignty of God.

It is helpful to compare the American Christian movement which developed out of these beginnings with the
constructive period in medieval faith.   In that earlier
time the Christian dialectic expressed itself in the monastic movement with its ever new beginnings, its multi-
tudinous and often divergent orders.   This *ecclesia* called
out of the world was in constant danger of abandoning
the common life which was the object of God's creative
and redemptive love.   The priestly church, on the other
hand, which lived for and in the world tended to lose its
distinctive gospel and to become the religious guardian of
established and sinful customs.   Only monasticism saved
it from acquiescence, petrifaction and complete loss of its
revolutionary character.   Monasticism in turn needed to
be brought back by reform after reform and the organization of ever new groups to the realization that the vision
of God required service.   As a result of these reforms but
also in response to the initial impetus toward God it became the builder of the church and the most effective
agency in the fashioning of medieval culture.   When
synthesis took the place of dialectic, and institution the
place of movement, the creative time was past.   The system of Thomas Aquinas and the corresponding hierarchical structure marked the death as much as they
signalized the fruition of medieval faith.   The same dialectic pattern worked itself out in America, where the

Christian movement could develop as freely as it had in unorganized Europe. Not in dependence on past examples and teachings, but in response to the vital demand of divine sovereignty, order after order of lay brothers and sisters separated itself for the sake of loyalty. These Pilgrims, Congregationalists, Quakers, Baptists, these Moravians, Dunkers, Mennonites, these Disciples and Christians — what are they but Protestant orders whose main principle is the kingdom rather than the vision of God? And Methodist preachers, with their saddlebags and books of discipline, are Franciscans or Dominicans in a new incarnation. As the monastic church-out-of-the-world became the builder of the church-in-the-world so the separatist church-against-the-world became the constructive church-for-the-world. Without design but in logical consequence of the faith in divine sovereignty the Protestant attempt to build the church in America turned into a movement following, though as from afar, the way of the living God.

IV. The Limitation of Power

A third principle which guided the constructive work of faith in America was the rule of limitation of all human power. The only ultimate answer to the universal tendency of finite power to exalt and absolutize itself lay, it was recognized, in redemption, but short of a final harmonization of all powers restraint was necessary.

John Cotton stated the principle as the Puritans understood it when he wrote:

Let all the world learn to give mortall men no greater power than they are content they shall use, for use it they will. . . . It is necessary . . . that all power that is on earth be limited, church-power or other. . . . It is counted a matter of danger to the state to limit prerogatives, but it is a further danger not to have them limited. They will be like a Tempest if they be not limited. A Prince himselfe can not tell where he will confine himself, nor can the people tell. . . . It is therefore fit for every man to be studious of the bounds which the Lord hath set; and for the People, in whom fundamentally all power lyes, to give as much power as God in his word gives to men.[36]

The principle was theocratic rather than democratic, despite Cotton's reference to the power of the people. This fact is best indicated in the *Model of Church and Civil Power* which stated that it is a " prerogative proper to God to require obedience of the sons of men." Hence the magistrate's power to make laws was confined to such " as either are expressed in the word of God in Moses's judicials — to wit sofar as they are of general and moral equity, and so binding all nations in all ages — to be deducted by way of general consequence and proportion from the word of God." Further, " in civil and indifferent things " the magistrate " hath no power given him of God to make what laws he please," for the will of no man is a rule of right unless it first be a right rule. Laws made in this sphere must commend themselves to reason.[37] Roger Williams agreed wholeheartedly with this statement insofar as it was negative, desiring only to have it applied consistently where matters of conscience were involved.

Theocracy implied the limitation of the civil power whether the form of government was monarchic, aristocratic, democratic or mixed. Despite the general tendency toward democracy, which was connected with the idea of the reign of Christ, there were endless disputes among early American Protestants about the question of civil government; but again there was fundamental agreement upon the point that if democracy were chosen it was subject to the same limitation by divine rule as any other form of government. The Puritans were suspicious of power in the hands of kings, aristocrats, priests and churches; by the same token they were suspicious of power in the hands of the people. Cotton and Hooker agreed with Williams and Penn that the people were the last mundane source of political power, yet it was theirs by God's allowance and " must not be exercised according to their humors, but according to the blessed will and law of God." [38] " In a free state no magistrate hath power over the bodies, goods, lands, liberties of a free people, but by their free consents." Free men, however, were not " free lords of their own estates, but are only stewards unto God, therefore they may not give their free consents to any magistrate to dispose of their bodies, goods, lands, liberties, at large as themselves please, but as God, the sovereign Lord of all, alone." [39] Shepard expressed the suspicion of democratic power when he reminded the people that they were corrupt and unstable, " apt to be led by colours, like birds by glasses and larkes by lures, and golden pretences which Innovators ever have." [40]   In the same spirit Winthrop contrasted natural and civil liberty, warning men against the former as the " wild beast, which all the ordinances of God are bent against, to restrain and subdue it," and defining the latter as a " liberty to that only which is good, just and honest," which is limited, moreover, by the covenant between God and man, by moral law and " the politic covenants and constitutions among men themselves." [41]   To a great extent Roger Williams and the Quakers shared this principle of the limitation of sovereignty even when the people were the sovereigns, as is often forgotten when the theocratic convictions of both Puritans and separatists are interpreted as a mere screen behind which priestly autocrats and lay democrats carried on their struggle.   Williams indeed conceded that there was a relative civil or moral goodness independent of godliness,[42] but with the Quakers he was fundamentally interested in providing inner restraints to the human abuse of power.   Neither he nor they were exponents of the idea of the autonomy of the " natural " man.

The principle of limitation of power was subject to abuse, of course, in the interest of whatever power happened to be in control.   Yet the religious conviction was real and was strong enough, as in the case of the church, to enforce limitation upon the self.   Like all moral principles it could be used for self-defense, but it was also used for self-criticism and self-limitation.   In many ways this doctrine that God alone was sovereign and that therefore all human exercise of power needed to be limited became a profound influence in American life, even when its sources were forgotten. "Someone has said," Lord Bryce wrote,

that the American government and Constitution are based on the theology of Calvin and the philosophy of Hobbes. This at least is true, that there is a hearty Puritanism in the view of human nature which pervades the instrument of 1787. It is the work of men who believed in original sin, and were resolved to leave open for transgressors no door which they could possibly shut. Compare this spirit with the enthusiastic optimism of the Frenchmen of 1789. It is not merely a difference of race temperaments: it is a difference of fundamental ideas. . . . The aim of the Constitution seems to be not so much to attain great common ends by securing a good government as to avert the evils which will flow, not merely from a bad government, but from any government strong enough to threaten the pre-existing communities or the individual citizen.[43]

Bryce is probably right in emphasizing the importance of the negative idea of original sin, but this idea is inseparable from the conviction that God is truly sovereign and that human power not only must but can be limited in the kingdom of God.

How much American democracy owed at this point to the Quakers rather than to the Puritans is intimated by Henry Adams, who assigns to the Pennsylvanians a leading role in the Jeffersonian period of American life. "To politics," he wrote, "the Pennsylvanians did not take kindly. Perhaps their democracy was so deep an instinct that they knew not what to do with political power when they gained it; as though political power were aristocratic in its nature, and democratic power a contradiction in terms." [44]   It was, one may suspect, not an instinct of democracy but the social heritage derived from Quakers and other sectarians which asserted itself in the Pennsylvania spirit.   These groups recognized that legal power was necessary for curbing unregenerate power, and therefore agreed to civil government; but since the exercise of power tended to corrupt men and to make them usurpers of the sovereignty of God the desire for power needed to be eliminated at its source.   Bryce and Adams suggest how differently the two groups of American Protestants employed the principle of limitation of power, but also how much they agreed on the idea itself.   The Puritan sought limitation by means of constitutionalism, the Scriptures and " politic covenants " and by the dispersion of power; [45] the separatist and the Quaker sought it by learning the humility of Christ.   Though both ways led to a kind of democracy it was democracy of a sort different from that which marched under the banner of the sovereignty of man.   It was democracy subject to the kingdom of God.

The principle of limitation was applicable to every finite reality, not to the state alone.   It is as much a mistake to make these Protestants, especially the Puritans, exponents of the absolute power of the church or the conscience as to make them early representatives of the claims of absolute popular sovereignty.   The great usurpation of the kingdom which belonged only to God had taken place, they all believed, in the church.   Ecclesiasticism stood in their eyes as monarchism, high capitalism and nationalism stood in the eyes of later generations.[46] With that great usurpation in mind they feared ecclesiastical absolutism more than anything else. Hence John Cotton proclaimed:

> Let it be a seasonable advertisement to all (if I were to speak to Princes) to all Princes, but however to all magistrates, how to make use of their authority to be as Protectors of the church, & in respect of their spirituall estate as children of the church, but not to give the horns to the church (though horns be for beauty and strength:) you see it makes the church a monster, and it is to make a beast of the church: and so if you should make Church Officers Justices of Peace, or counsellors, or prostitute your own government to them, that if the Church condemn any, then you must do so to . . . ; and this puts your Horns upon the churches unto monstrous deformity, therefore it is necessary for Magistrates to keep their power in their own hands, and not to take things *Ipso facto* from the Church.

"There is nothing more disproportionall to us," he goes on to say, "than to affect Supremacy, for us to wear the Horns that might push kings, to throw down any, or to desire Magistrates to execute what we shall think fit, verily it is not compatible to the simplicity of the Church of Christ. Neither may they give their power to us, nor may we take it from them." [47] To give civil power to the church is to give it "not the key of the kingdom of heaven, but the key of the bottomlesse pit." [48] The careful distinction between the powers of church and state which the New Englanders sought to enforce was inspired no less by the desire to limit the church than by the wish to limit the civic power. In all of this they were following Calvin and other reformers who had protested against the exercise of dominion by the church in the same breath with which they declared its independence. Hence also ministers were prohibited the exercise of civil office.

Williams and the Quakers again went further along the path taken by the Puritans. The first sought only greater consistency in conduct than the caution of Massachusetts Bay leaders allowed. To give civil power to the church was to overturn and root up " the very foundations and roots of all true Christianity, and absolutely denying the Lord Jesus, the Great Anointed, to be yet come into the flesh." [49] The only power which the church could claim without suffering corruption was the power of the " two-edged sword of God's spirit," the power of suffering, of being persecuted, the power made perfect in weakness. This also was the fundamental position of the Quakers who with Williams prepared the way for the separation of church and state because they loved the church and sought to keep it free from the taint of power.

The adoption of congregational and associational types of church organization was due in part at least to this principle of limitation. " Leave every church Independent," said Cotton; " not Independent from brotherly Counsell, God forbid it that we should refuse that; but when it comes to power, that one Church shall have power over the rest, then look for a Beast. . . . Amplitude of dominion was never a note of the Church of

Christ since the world began." [50] The restriction of the power of the keys to the congregation was a measure adopted quite as much in the interest of limiting church power as in that of asserting the rights of the local church. The congregation further was prevented from becoming a " Beast " by being subjected to the rule of the covenant and of the Scriptures, and by the dispersion of power between elders and brethren who checked each other. It is true, of course, that in this area of church organization another idea entered — the idea of the kingdom of Christ, which must be dealt with later on; yet the principle of divine sovereignty and the determination that this power should not be usurped by any finite reality were important also.

God's kingship limited conscience as well as the church, for the conscience of man was not an absolute. It was the principle in man whereby he understood the absolute law. Conscience, Ames had said, is

a mans judgment of himself according to the judgment of God of him. . . . Through the goodness of God the knowledge of many things which wee ought to doe or shun is still conserved in man's mind after the fall. . . . This Synteresis differs only in respect or apprehension from the Law of Nature or from that Law of God which is naturally written in the hearts of all men, for the law is the object and synteresis is the object apprehended.[51]

Doubtless it was always wrong for a man to go against his conscience, and Puritans agreed with Quakers and separatists in principle that " there is no man, no not the king, that hath coercive power over conscience." Yet this subjective principle was subordinate to the objective. Not conscience but the reality which conscience apprehended was absolute. The Quaker realized the relative character of conscience no less than did the New England theocrat, recognized that it was hardened by fleshly wisdom and defiled by disobedience, that it needed to keep itself free of offense by obedience to the light of Christ.[52] Again the problem of doing complete justice to the relative sovereignty of a finite power caused many difficulties and conflicts, but no Protestant sought to solve them by simply identifying conscience with the rule of God.

The principle of limitation, finally, had its application to the economic life. In recent years the thesis that Protestantism was the nurse if not the parent of capitalism has been widely adopted. Yet the distinction between the Protestant principle of the kingdom of God and the principle of laissez faire economics is quite as great and of the same sort as the difference between the former and the ideal of political liberalism. The faith in the kingdom did not demand that unconverted man with his lust for power and gain be liberated, but rather that he be brought into willing subjection to the rule of God. Atheism of the practical sort found in Deism needed to intervene before this idea could be confounded with economic liberalism. The fear of human usurpation of divine power led, indeed, to the limitation of church and state, and the fact that such limitation might allow an economic absolutism to arise was not clearly foreseen, just as in Europe early

Protestants did not foresee that the limitation of the church would give room for the rise of political absolutism. Yet the spirit of capitalism and the spirit of Protestantism remain two wholly different things.

When one looks at the way in which American Christians resisted the tendency toward economic expansionism, in Pennsylvania as in New England, one must conclude that they were not unaware of the necessity of limitation in this sphere as well as in others. With regard to this point Tawney does some justice to New England Puritanism:

> In that happy, bishopless Eden where men desired only to worship God " according to the simplicitie of the gospel and to be ruled by the laws of God's word," not only were " tobacco and immodest fashions and costly apparel " . . . forbidden to true professors, but the Fathers adopted toward that " notorious evil . . . whereby most men walked in all their commerce — to buy as cheap and to sell as dear as they can " an attitude which possibly would not be wholly congenial to their more businesslike descendants.[53]

In the distribution of land and in the efforts to regulate trade to which Cotton and Winthrop testify, the principle of limitation lest power and pride lead to rebellion against God's kingdom was followed. The Quaker doctrine of moderation in economic enterprise was even more strict. George Fox had preached to the economic man:

> Repent ye Merchants of London, repent, ye Merchants and great men of the city, the day of the Lord's hand is coming upon

you, the day of the Lord's wrath is to be poured upon you, who have lived in wickedness, fulness and gluttony, and serving the creature more than the Creator, who is God blessed forever. . . . Ye Tradesmen, . . . ye Watermen and Fishermen, . . . ye poorer sort of people, . . . all ye Husbandmen, . . . repent . . . and be turned unto the Lord, that your minds may be brought out of the greediness of gain.

All Friends everywhere that were shopkeepers, or merchants, or factors, or followed any trade were " to keep low in the power of God " and not to go beyond their capacity or reach after more than they could perform. William Penn had repeated this counsel of moderation and limitation in business and Quaker discipline enforced it.[54]

It remains true that while the principle was recognized as applicable to economics it was not implemented as was the case in the political and ecclesiastical spheres, where the dispersion and balancing of power provided for more than internal restraint. We have the right to believe that failure to organize the economic life in similar fashion was not due to hypocrisy but rather to the fact that the capitalism of the seventeenth and early eighteenth centuries was a relatively modest and harmless thing whose growth toward an absolutism like that which church and state had exercised could not be foreseen. The principle of divine sovereignty, not the idea of economic autonomy, remained the rule of Protestants here as elsewhere.

In these ways then, through insistence upon constitutionalism, upon the primacy and independence of the church, and upon the limitation of all human power, the faith in the kingdom of God became a constructive thing in early America. It brought forth a movement which had definite meaning and character despite the rich variety of its manifestations. Though Pilgrims, Puritans, Quakers and sectarians may have believed that in America they might construct a society of secure institutions in which to dwell until the end of time, their obedience to the sovereign God led them to produce something better — a life directed toward the infinite goal.

THE KINGDOM OF CHRIST

I. Spiritual Experiments

THE CHRISTIAN FAITH in the kingdom of God is a three-fold thing. Its first element is confidence in the divine sovereignty which, however hidden, is still the reality behind and in all realities. A second element is the conviction that in Jesus Christ the hidden kingdom was not only revealed in a convincing fashion but also began a special and new career among men, who had rebelled against the true law of their nature. The third element is the direction of life to the coming of the kingdom in power or to the redemption of the self-sufficient world. Professor A. E. Taylor has called attention to the fact that the three notes of God, grace and eternal life are characteristic of all advanced religion; these correspond upon the whole to the three characteristics of the Christian consciousness of the kingdom. Yet it must be noted that the latter is of a thoroughly historical character, interested in events and in the meaning of history.[1]

It was characteristic of the Protestant Reformation that in it, as in the Franciscan movement, all three elements became intensely real again to men. Which one predominated cannot be readily determined; now it seemed to be the note of sovereignty, now that of grace, now that of hope. Although in some groups one element took precedence over the others, yet all three were vividly present in all of the movements. Doubtless Quakers and separatists put grace ahead of sovereignty, while the Puritans may have inverted the relation; but as the former are unintelligible without recognition of their conviction of divine sovereignty, so the latter can be represented only in caricature if we leave their faith in the covenant of grace out of account. And the common conviction of all that the kingdom had begun a new career upon earth with Jesus Christ, had very great bearing on the type of individual and social life which they fostered or produced.

We may represent the conviction of the American Protestants in the familiar terms of revolution. They were convinced that a new beginning had been made in human history, that Roman Catholicism had lost the benefits of this revolution, and that the Reformation was the resumption of the revolutionary movement. But what had been the significance of the great change wrought in Jesus Christ as these Protestants saw it? Our time finds it as difficult to understand the vocabulary they used as future generations will discover to be the case when they read our ethical, economic and political arguments and inquire into the meaning of such terms as " value," " economic determinism," " revolution," " liberalism " and the like. Some interpreters, unable or unwilling to understand the symbols, hasten to conclude that there was no meaning in all the strife about gospel and law, or grace and sin, save the always intelligible meaning of the lust for power and the pride of place. Yet if we share the presuppositions of the Protestants we shall not find their conceptions too difficult to understand, nor the resultant arguments unintelligible. The common conviction was that whereas before the revolution of Jesus Christ men, with some exceptions, had to be kept in order and had to keep themselves in order by fear and restraint and were without hope, they now had experienced or could experience the " expulsive power of a new affection " which made a life of freedom possible. The new relation to God established by Jesus Christ meant that an order of liberty and love had been substituted for the order of regimentation and fear. The promise which God had fulfilled was the promise of the prophet Jeremiah:

Behold, the days come, saith the Lord, that I will make a new covenant with the house of Israel, and with the house of Judah; not according to the covenant that I made with their fathers in the day that I took them by the hand to bring them out of the land of Egypt; which my covenant they brake, although I was a husband unto them, saith the Lord. But this shall be the covenant that I will make with the house of Israel; After those days, saith the Lord, I will put my law in their inward parts, and write it in their hearts; and will be their God, and they shall be my people. And they shall teach no more every man his neighbor, and every man his brother, saying, Know the Lord; for they shall all know me, from the least of them unto the greatest of them, saith the Lord; for I will forgive their iniquity, and I will remember their sin no more.[2]

When early American Protestants thought of the promise, they did not think in the first place of a warless world wherein lions and lambs would lie down together, or of the plenty which every man might enjoy in tranquillity beneath his own vine and fig tree. They thought rather of the cleansing of the inward parts, of the restoration to man of inner harmony, and of the elimination of the war in the members, whence all other wars and fightings came. They thought of victory over the lust of the flesh, the lust of the eyes and the pride of life which, unconquered, made repression, coercion and the terror of the Lord necessary. They thought of a knowledge of God which was a complete conviction of mind and heart that God was God, man's complete and sole good. This knowledge was to be so complete that it would result in the doing of good for its own sake. Now the divine sovereign had fulfilled the promise of liberty, of freedom from coercion, for hearts who knew and willed the good alone. Separatists and Quakers were particularly aware of the revolution and of the actuality of the new order of grace. For them all things had become new. Their spirit was less one of trembling before Jehovah's awful throne than of rejoicing with the hundred and forty-four thousand in the presence of the lamb on Mount Zion. America has produced few more beautiful devotional books than Roger Williams' *Experiments of Spirituall Life and Health*, " penned and writ " for the most part, as he said, " in the thickest of the naked Indians of America, in their very wild houses, and by their barbarous fires." Its purpose, in the author's words, was "to fill each truly Christian soule with triumph and rejoycing," and to speak "peace and joy to the Weakest Lamb and Child" in Christianity.[3] It is more like the Williams of the Winthrop letters than like the author of the *Bloudy Tenent*. It reveals a man who was concerned with the law written on the inward parts of those who, poor in spirit, hungered and thirsted after a true goodness and found it offered to them by the revolution inaugurated by Jesus Christ.

The revolutionary consciousness of the Quakers was even more pronounced. They were more interested in the kingdom of Christ than in the sovereignty of God; that is to say, they were impressed even more by the fact that the kingdom had come and could come to men in their own lives, bringing liberty and joy, than by the fact that universal law and justice reigned throughout the spheres. Fox's great *apologia pro vita sua* bears witness on every page to this revolutionary idea, above all, perhaps, in the statement of his commission recorded in the *Journal*:

I was sent to turn people from darkness to the light, that they might receive Christ Jesus; for, to as many as should receive him in his light, I saw that he would give power to become the sons of God, which I had obtained by receiving Christ. I was to direct people to the spirit that gave forth the Scriptures, by which they might be led into all truth. . . . I was to turn them to the grace of God, and to the truth in the heart, which came by Jesus; that by his grace they might be taught, which would bring them salvation, that their hearts might be established by it, their words might be seasoned, and all might come to know their salvation nigh. For I saw that Christ had died for all men, and was a propitiation for all, and enlightened all men and women with his divine and saving light; and that none could be true believers but who believed in it.[4]

Dewsbury and Pennington stated the idea of the new covenant even more clearly.[5] The difference between the Quakers and their opponents, who were yet their comrades, lay in the radical fashion in which the former believed in the newness of life and in the universality of the Christian revolution.

The Antinomians of Boston had been earlier representatives of this same type of mind. For they also believed that the new life, the establishment of God's law in the heart by love, was of such a sort that Christ lived in the Christian. They believed, therefore, that the Christian pilgrimage did not pursue the way of moralistic endeavor, but rather followed the road of divine forgiveness and of liberty and faith.[6]

When Puritanism is regarded from a point of view which magnifies its conflict with separatism, it seems as though it had been exclusively interested in law while separatists loved liberty, or that the former believed in the sovereignty of God and was conservative while the latter sought the kingdom of Christ and had confidence in the Christian life. Yet Puritans were almost as convinced as were their rivals that in Christ all things had become new. Though the sense of divine sovereignty took a certain precedence in their thought over faith in the kingdom of Christ, it was not completely predominant. If one has had the story of New England legalism dinned into his ears and then goes to hear the old Puritan preachers, one is struck by the clearness of the evangelical note.[7] The negative ethics of restraint is doubtless emphatically sounded by John Cotton, but there is an even stronger note — the assurance of grace, the belief in the fulfillment of the promise " that he will write his laws in our hearts; that he will forgive our sins, and remember our iniquities no more; that we shall know him." [8]

Thomas Shepard was regarded by the Antinomians as the best of " the legall preachers " but still a legalist. Yet we may put his *Meditations and Spiritual Experiences* alongside Williams' *Spirituall Experiments*. It also is concerned with Christ and the soul's relation to him, and it bears witness to a humility that was genuine and to a love that sought to be pure. In his *Sincere Convert* Shepard writes of the love of Christ in the following lyric terms:

As 'tis with Woman when the fulnesse of the Husband's love is seen, it knits the heart invincibly to him, and makes her do anything for him; so here. And as we say of Trees, if the Tree begins to wither and dye, the only way is . . . water the root. Love is the next root of all Grace. Love Christ and you will never be weary of doing for Christ; love him, and he will love you. Now what kindles love so much as this comprehending knowledge of the Lord Jesus, and his love; this will make a man a burning Beacon of love; make a man melt into love which is as strong as death — much water cannot quench it. Faith is our feet whereby we come to Christ, Love our hand whereby we work for Christ.[9]

It was Increase Mather who stated the situation in which doubtless many of the other preachers found themselves: "*Knowing the Terror of the Lord, I seek to persuade you by those Arguments; nevertheless I take no pleasure to tell you thereof.* But now that I am speaking to you of the pardoning grace of God, me-thinks I am in my element." [10]

These men knew indeed the terror of the Lord. They knew as Paul had known that man's choice did not lie simply between law and liberty but between law, liberty and lust, and that the way of liberty lay along an exceedingly narrow path between the abysses of restraint and anarchy. There was hearty agreement upon the fundamental point among all the Protestants. The kingdom of God is not a reign of terror but one of love, not of law but of liberty. God has willed to reconcile men to his will, to write his law upon their hearts, and he has done this by means of Jesus Christ. He who has become a citizen of the true kingdom of Christ, or of the invisible church, is free. He does good, he executes justice, he loves his neighbor, he has public spirit, not because he is constrained by external laws and sanctions, but because he is no longer concerned about himself and can love goodness for its own sake.

As all revolutionary parties are bound to do, the various groups in Protestantism disagreed on the completeness of this revolution. Separatists tended toward perfectionism, believing more or less that one who had entered into the kingdom of Christ was now wholly good and could therefore be wholly free. The more cautious Puritans asserted that

when God converts a sinner, and translates him into the state of grace, he freeth him from his natural bondage under sin, and by his grace alone inables him freely to will and to do that which is spiritually good; yet so, as that by reason of his remaining corruption, he doth not perfectly nor onely will that which is good, but doth also will that which is evil. The will of man is made perfectly and immutably free to good alone in the state of Glory onely.[11]

They insisted, therefore, that the citizen of the kingdom of Christ continued to require discipline. In the upshot the separatists practically agreed with them, for they also exercised a careful restraint upon one another in their conventicles. Moreover, they speedily discovered that since the revolution had not come to all men the restraints of civil government continued to be necessary in the social life. The common motto of both right and left wing Christian revolutionaries was Paul's frequently quoted advice to the Phillipians, " Brethren, ye have been called to liberty, only use not your liberty as an occasion to the flesh but in love serve one another."

The conviction that under the sovereignty of God a new era had begun with Christ and that its meaning lay in the liberty of men who had accepted the yoke of the kingdom and had found it easy, was of primary importance throughout constructive Protestantism for the or-

ganization of religious societies. The true invisible
church was made up of those who had become members
of the kingdom of Christ and the visible church was to
imitate as best it might both the purity and the freedom
of the invisible. The church was to be the church of free
men in Christ. Said Hooker:

> These are the times when people shall be fitted for such
> priviledges, fit I say to obtain them and fit to use them. Fit to
> obtain them at Gods hands for . . . people shall run to and fro,
> and knowledge shall increase; they shall by the strength of their
> desires, improve the most painful exercise of their thoughts, in
> the most serious search of the mystery of godlinesse, and bloud-
> houndlike, who are bent upon their prey, they shall most inde-
> fatigably trace the truth . . . and thus digging for wisdom as
> for hid treasures, and seeking the Lord and his will, with their
> whole heart, they shall finde him, and understand it. Fit to use
> them, now the Lord will write his laws in their hearts, and put
> it into their inward parts.[12]

More cautiously John Cotton described the situation
when he wrote:

> The *Saints* (in these knowing times) finding that the *Key of
> Knowledge* hath so farre opened their hearts, that they see with
> their owne eyes into the substantialls of Godlinesse, and that
> through the instruction and guidance of their teachers, they are
> enabled to understand for themselves such other things as they
> are to joyn in the practice of. They doe therefore further (many
> of them) begin more than to suspect, that some share in the
> *Key of power* should likewise appertain to them.[13]

The same caution which made the Puritan wing mate
liberty with restraint in other spheres operated here, so

that dispersion of power between elders and saints seemed desirable, while greater equality and liberty prevailed among separatists. But the principle of liberty was clearly recognized in the congregational organization of the church which prevailed in both groups. It was recognized further in the right of the churches to choose their own pastors, to frame their own covenant, to exercise discipline and to accept or reject candidates for membership.

It has often been noted that this church democracy became a school of political democracy. What needs to be emphasized even more is that the whole outlook on life which lay back of church democracy was one which definitely looked toward liberty in all the relations of life. The Protestants of the seventeenth century were consciously embarked upon a permanent revolution which was to continue until complete freedom was brought in by the " Order of Glory." The liberalism of this Protestantism was not of the sort which made liberty a presupposition or a self-evident right of man; freedom was its goal. Its presupposition was the human bondage to sin; it was thoroughly convinced that no liberty could last or be beneficial which was not the liberty of men who had been brought somehow to fall in love with a universal goodness and to love it for its own sake alone. The permanent revolution in which they were engaged was designed to make men fit for ever greater freedom. They all agreed that this end could not be achieved by the education of the intellect alone, much as Puritans prized learning. A rebirth of the whole man was required, a revolution in the will to power or in the will to live. All too often when they are regarded from the standpoint of a later, secularized liberalism, the similarity of their presuppositions as well as the identity of their aims is forgotten, and they are forced into the divisive categories of philosophies which were not their own.

II. THE REIGN OF CHRIST AND THE GREAT REVIVAL

The idea of the kingdom of Christ which had remained secondary in the first period of the more orthodox Protestant development in America became the dominant idea when, after a period of institutionalization, the dynamic faith in the kingdom reasserted itself in the Great Awakening and in the series of revivals which, from Edwards to Finney and beyond, influenced the whole of American life. The Awakening was not simply a repristination of seventeenth century Protestantism. Though it was definitely continuous with the earlier movement, it faced a new society with new problems and represented a new emphasis. It arose in the new world of emancipated individuals who had become their own political masters to an uncommon degree. It dealt, in America particularly, with men and families who through the acquisition of free or cheap land had been made economically independent. It confronted men who were being intellectually emancipated from the dogmas of the past by the filtering down into the common life of ideas developed by scientists and philosophers. It spoke to people who had been freed to no small extent from the bonds of customary morality by the recognition that it was largely pragmatic in origin and, even more, by the relaxation of group pressure upon men and families in new settlements or in widely separated homesteads. Absolute individuals had replaced absolute kings and absolute churches.

The *Letters of Crèvecœur* describe the attitude which was fostered in American colonists by the new conditions: "Here the rewards of his industry follow with equal steps in the progress of his labor; his labor is founded on the basis of nature, *self-interest:* can it want a stronger allurement?" Of the sober farmers in the "middle settlements" he writes that

as freemen they will be litigious; pride and obstinacy are often the cause of lawsuits; the nature of our laws and government may be another. . . . As farmers they will be anxious and careful to get as much as they can, because what they get is theirs. . . . As Christians, religion curbs them not in their opinions; the laws inspect our actions; our thoughts are left to God. Industry, good living, selfishness, litigiousness, country politics, the pride of freemen, religious indifference, are their characteristics.[14]

This temper of practical individualism or of "Yankee rationalism" rather than the Arminian theology or Deistic philosophy of the time challenged the Christian movement in America.

Not only was the situation different from that of the seventeenth century but the religious response to it was primarily in terms of the kingdom of Christ rather than in those of the sovereignty of God. The emphasis which had been represented by Quakers and separatists in the early period now became dominant. The traditionally minded continued, of course, to deal with the new situation by means of restraint and the limitation of power, but the " new lights " and " new schools " which made the idea of regeneration primary represented the constructive religious movement of the period from Great Awakening to Civil War.

It is noteworthy, however, that just as the early Quakers had kept their theory of the Christian revolution closely related to their faith in the sovereignty of God so the Evangelicals now presupposed or reaffirmed the rule of God as the basis of all they believed about the kingdom of Christ. Jonathan Edwards, the greatest theologian of the movement, comes to mind at once as one in whom faith in regeneration was solidly founded upon a supreme conviction of the reality of divine sovereignty. It would be difficult to find in all religious literature a more moving confession of loyalty to the kingdom of God than the one in his *Personal Narrative*, or to discover more illuminating statements of the principle than those which abound in his writings.[15] In his thought faith in divine sovereignty was the explicit foundation of the kingdom of Christ; for the other leaders of the movement it was at least implicitly so. Wesley's essential Calvinism — if this belief be Calvinism — has recently been described by Professor Cell,[16] though it may be that the great Methodist's limitation lay at the point of his frequent unawareness of this presupposition of his gospel. For Whitefield and the

Tennents, for Archibald Alexander and later on for Finney, faith in the divine sovereignty was the platform on which they stood as they preached the kingdom of Christ.[17]   The staunch Baptist leader Isaac Backus shared their fundamental conviction.   The greatest Quaker of the Awakening period was doubtless John Woolman.   In spirit he is nearer to Edwards than any other man of the time, aware always, like the latter, of his infinite dependence upon the " Incomprehensible Being " by whose " breath the flame of life was kindled in all Animal and Sensible creatures." [18]

The fundamental importance of the sovereignty of God to the revival movement becomes apparent, however, only when we ask what its preachers meant when they exhorted men to press into the kingdom or when, as in the case of gentle Woolman, they persuaded them to take on the meekness of the Lord.   The kingdom of Christ for them was decidedly not a society of altruists who had freely chosen to live for the benefit of their neighbors, nor was it an association of idealists who had come together for the sake of promoting self and social culture.   They were all aware that man's altruism and idealism are not only unreliable but also in the nature of the human case bound to the chariot of self-interest, so that they easily become subterfuges of the will to power and of self-assertion.   They knew that the problem of human life was not the discovery of an adequate ideal nor the generation of will power whereby ideals might be realized, but rather the redirection of the will to live and the liberation of the drive in human life from the inhibitions of fear, conflict and the sense of futility.[19]   They saw that the human will is always committed to something and that so long as it is not committed to the universal good it is attached to the relative.   The will, said Edwards, is as its strongest motive is.[20]   " In all such offerings, something is virtually worshiped, and whatever it is, be it self, or our fellow men, or the world, *that* is allowed to usurp the place that should be given to God, and to receive the offerings that should be made to him." [21] Life never begins in a vacuum of freedom, but awakes to its tacit commitments.   It is always loyal to something and its problem is how to transfer its loyalty from the ephemeral, the partial, and the relative, which by assuming absoluteness become devilish, to the eternal, universal and truly absolute.   Only the action of God himself is sufficient to effect the transfer, and so the divine sovereignty stands at the gate of the kingdom of Christ.   Unless it opens the portals they remain closed and closed the tighter because man presses against them in the wrong direction.

The divine sovereignty, according to the Awakeners, is fundamental to the kingdom of Christ in a second way. God has acted and is acting in history; in Jesus Christ he has brought in the great change which has opened to men the kingdom of liberty and love.   And, in the third place, the nature of that divine event with its repetition in the lives of believers is reconciliation to Being, to the divine reality, which man cannot but consider to be his enemy so long as he is intent upon promoting his own will and life.

In these ways the proclamation of the kingdom of Christ was solidly based upon the conviction of God's kingship, more solidly, if possible, than the communist doctrine of revolution is based upon the materialist theory of history or the art of healing upon the knowledge of anatomy and the conviction of nature's dependable uniformity.

It is evident that the kingdom of Christ into which the revivalists bade men press in dependence on God's grace was not identified with the visible church. It was more than ever the invisible church, and the preachers, ordained and lay, resembled more than ever the friars of the twelfth and thirteenth centuries. Churches arose out of the movement — Methodist, Baptist, Cumberland Presbyterian and many others; established churches were strengthened — the Congregational, the Presbyterian, the Episcopalian and the Society of Friends. But the object of the movement was not the strengthening of institutional religion. Neither was it the enforcement of codes, of restrictive laws against Sabbath breaking, luxury, adultery, drunkenness and other major or minor vices. To be sure some parts of the movement, such as, for instance, the reform movement carried on under the auspices of the standing order in Connecticut, tended in this direction and when the revivals went to seed in the later nineteenth century restraint and law took the place of liberty and promise. The essence of the great movement under the great leaders, however, was no more restrictive than it was institutional.

The kingdom of Christ was understood first of all as it had been in the seventeenth century. It was the rule of self-restraint in lives which had become repentant of their evil tendency. That tendency was brought home to them by the recognition that the continued crucifixion of the Son of God is as much the result of human morality as of human immorality. Repentance meant the crucifixion of the will to power no matter how nobly it might disguise itself. It meant the beginning though not the perfection of humility, which was not cultivated as an excellence but borne as a fruit of knowledge. The kingdom of Christ was the rule of sincerity in lives which had been made to understand the deviousness and trickery of the well loved ego as it skulks and hides in the labyrinthine ways of the mind, and which, having been made to see that they lived by forgiveness and not merit, needed no longer to defend themselves against themselves, their fellow men and God. The kingdom of Christ was the liberty of those who had received some knowledge of the goodness of God and who reflected in their lives the measure of their knowledge and devotion.

What distinguished the Evangelical view and made it an advance on the ideas of previous Protestantism was the insistence that the reign of Christ was above all a rule of knowledge in the minds of men. The Quakers had long identified the " seed of the spirit " with truth; the kingdom of Christ was one of enlightenment. This testimony they now renewed. Edwards sought to convince the mind rather than to stir the emotions and was genuinely surprised at the display of " religious affections " which followed some of his stiffly logical preaching. " Converting influences," he wrote, " very commonly bring an extraordinary conviction of the reality and certainty of the great things of religion; though in some this is much greater some time after conversion than at first." Some are unable to explain their convictions but probably " they have intuitively beheld, and immediately felt, most illustrious and powerful evidence of divinity " in the Christian truths. " I suppose the grounds of such a conviction of the truth of divine things to be just and rational; but yet, in some God makes use of their own reason much more sensibly than in others. Oftentimes persons have (so far as could be judged) received the first saving conviction from reasoning which they have heard from the pulpit; and often in the course of reasoning they are led into their own meditations." [22]

For Wesley the heart of faith was immediate knowledge, not in the mystic sense of union with God but in the empirical sense of personal awareness of the operation of God in life and human history. Archibald Alexander, foremost Presbyterian theologian of the revival, described conversion, regeneration and sanctification primarily in terms of enlightenment.

Every man on whom this divine operation has passed experiences *new views of divine truth*. The soul sees in these things *that* which it never saw before. It discerns in the truth of God a beauty and excellence of which it had no conception until now. . . . Of necessity there must be . . . endless variety in the particular views of new converts; but still they all partake of new views of divine truth; and the same truths will be generally contemplated, sooner or later; but not in the same order, nor exhibited to all with the same degree of clearness. Now according to the views which I entertain, this spiritual knowledge granted to the regenerated soul is nothing else but saving faith; for knowledge and belief involve each other.[23]

Finney follows Edwards, observing that "regeneration is nothing else than the will being duly influenced by truth. There may be and often are many providences concerned in enlightening the mind and in inducing regeneration. These are instrumentalities. They are means or instruments of presenting the truth. Mercies, judgments, men, measures and in short all those things that conduce to enlightening the mind, are instrumentalities employed in affecting it." [24] The revivalists took very seriously the promise that "they shall all know me," and their interest in Christian truths was not in their pragmatic value; rather it was in their truth.

Yet it is evident that the kingdom of Christ was not to be entered into merely by taking thought. The leaders of the religious enlightenment were rationalists — if logical and intense use of the reason may be called rationalism — but they were aware that reason can operate only on the basis of presuppositions prior to all logical processes. They differed from the humanist rationalists of their day not in rejecting reason but in refusing the presuppositions of humanism and in making the presuppositions of the Christian revelation their own. Yet they belonged to the empiricist movement more than to the rationalistic one. Reason, as they employed it, not only acknowledged its presuppositions but worked upon and within the stuff of experience. To what sort of experience, then, might one look for verification and insight into the truth of the gospel? Gospel experience alone could convince of gospel truth. Doubtless the leaders involved themselves in the dilemmas of empiricism: the reproduction of the experiment necessarily implied the arrangement of conditions under which it could succeed; it required previous faith in its successful outcome; and if an experiment failed it might always be said that the correct procedure had not been rigorously followed. Moreover, the tendency to see God at work only within the sphere of religious experience came to have fateful consequences. Nevertheless the empirical and experimental method brought thousands to see the actual truth and importance of ideas which had come to have only a stale existence in books, sermons and creeds. They apprehended the truth of the gospel as not one truth among many, but as the fundamental truth which made a profound difference. It had become " saving truth " or " saving knowledge."

In this emphasis upon immediate experience of God in his kingdom the Christian enlightenment carried on and developed the principles of earlier Protestantism in two respects. In the first place, it undertook in the face of the new necessity the tremendous task of teaching the multitudes of emancipated individuals in foreign countries as well as at home, whereas earlier Protestantism had tended to confine itself to the religious institutions. In the second place, it developed the Reformation's paradoxical doctrine of the Word of God, in which the problem of external and internal authority had been stated. As we have seen, in the dialectic between the objective criterion of the Word of God in Scriptures and the subjective criterion of the testimony of the Holy Spirit orthodoxy had tended to emphasize the former, separatism the latter, while each needed to recognize the principle represented by the other. In the Awakening the two principles were combined. Practically, the Awakening stimulated very great interest in and reading of the Scriptures while insisting upon the necessity of personal experience of the truth taught in Scriptures. Theoretically, Wesley, Edwards and their colleagues maintained the principle of divine initiative in revelation and of the objective criterion by which all personal experience needed to be judged, while holding at the same time that the objective needed to become subjective, the historical contemporary. If we may adapt a later philosophical formula we can state their general position thus: Scripture without experience is empty, but experience without Scripture is blind. Hence, though they used the Bible with far greater freedom than their immediate orthodox predecessors had done, they used it with greater fidelity and keener recognition of the problem involved than had the exponents of the " inner light." [25]

In describing the reign of Christ as a rule of the knowledge of God, we have left out of account an element which was a great asset as well as a great liability to the Awakening and the revivals — the emotional factor. The "religious affections" which were called forth by the preaching of Edwards, Whitefield and other American "friars" were unexpected, by the early leaders at least. The wails and groans, the shouts of joy, the physical prostrations and more vivid phenomena of hysteria, which in the decline of the movement came to be highly valued, were regarded by its opponents as damning evidence of its perversity and caused the more thoughtful of its leaders no little concern. Their orthodox predecessors as well as the sober Deists had taught them to be suspicious of all enthusiasm. The attitude was due not only to reaction against the wild religions of civil war and Commonwealth days but also to the desire of bourgeois society to hold at a distance all influences which might disturb the tight, complacent self-sufficiency of life and thought in a world that had been made safe for the Philistine democracy of the early eighteenth century. The new groups of proletarians in England and of frontiersmen in America, however, were by no means content with the safe structure of practical or intellectual rationalism in which the satisfied had fortified themselves. They were no foes to enthusiasm nor were they insulated against new convictions. When these convictions took hold of them they responded with their whole nature. When they saw the reality of an order of being other than that walled and

hemmed-in existence in which a stale institutional religion and bourgeois rationalism were content to dwell,
they responded emotionally rather than intellectually,
even as the romanticists of the same period embraced with
emotion the nature which had been held at arm's length
by rationalists. It was all very unrefined and disturbing.
Inevitable excesses and exuberances repelled those who
admired decency and established order more than life.
The greatness of the revival leaders appeared in their
open-minded recognition that if emotional response was
not a guarantee of sincerity, or physical manifestation a
proof of authentic conversion, neither were they evidences of speciousness.[26] Doubtless tests of sincerity and
truth needed to be sought elsewhere than in the emotions; yet truth which was not merely true by reference to
some impersonal standard but " truth for me " required
for its apprehension as well as for its expression the activity of a whole man, of intellect and will, of mind and
body. It was an affair not only of existential judgment —
as theologians learned to say later — but of value judgment also. Divine reality, whatever else it was, was also
a value, which could not be effectively apprehended save
as the inclination of the whole man was directed toward
it. " If we be not in good earnest in religion, and our wills
and inclinations be not strongly exercised, we are nothing," said Edwards. " The things of religion are so great
that there can be no suitableness in the exercises of our
hearts, to their nature and importance, unless they be
lively and powerful." [27] Yet these exercises of the heart,

these motions of approval and disapproval, of love and hatred, which are affairs of emotion and of will, " are not heat without light; but evermore arise from some information of the understanding, some spiritual instruction that the mind receives, some light or actual knowledge. . . . Knowledge is the key that first opens the hard heart, enlarges the affections, and opens the way for men into the kingdom of heaven." [28]

In their new way the Evangelicals thus made effective and explicit the Protestant principle that God and faith belong together, or that a knowledge of God which is conceptual only and not axiological is not really knowledge at all, or that, to use a different symbolism, a knowledge which is that of the head and not of the heart is of little importance in religion. At the same time they understood that this knowledge which is faith, or this faith which is knowledge, is available to the common man as readily as to the scholar living in his conceptual world. It is even more available to the ordinary person in whom the pride of the intellect and the defense of established categories offer no such resistance to the revelation of God as these do in theological and philosophical minds. The kingdom of Christ remains then a rule of knowledge. To be a member of this kingdom is to be one who sees the excellency and the beauty of God in Christ, and so loves him with all his heart for his own sake alone.

Such knowledge requires activity. The kingdom of Christ is the kingdom of love, and love is not only an emotion; it is a tendency to action, or action itself.[29] To love God is to obey him; the knowing of the good is the doing of the good. Edwards above all, but the other revival leaders also, followed in the train of seventeenth century Puritans, and went beyond them, in seeking evidence of true faith in its fruits in action. They said " love," whereas the Puritans had said " holiness "; they apprehended the whole world as the sphere of action even more than their predecessors had done; they thought more in terms of man's nonprofessional relations to his fellow men than in those of the calling. Yet they carried forward the earlier interests and applied them to the new conditions in the new time in effective fashion.

In preaching the kingdom of Christ as the kingdom of love they did not commit the mistake their successors often made, that of defining love of neighbor as the essence of Christianity, as though men could practice this love without reference to other elements in the Christian life, without apprehension of the divine sovereignty or without revolutionary change from natural to divine affection. Neither did they fall into the other error of confusing love with amiable sentiment. Sentiment which does not press to practice is like knowledge which does not issue in action; if the latter is the abhorred speculative knowledge, that is, spectator knowledge, the former is counterfeit affection, satisfied with itself and not based on knowledge of reality.[30] Practice is the test of genuine love. As Edwards said: " Love is an active principle; a principle that we always find is active in things of this world. . . . Reason teaches that a man's actions are the

most proper test and evidence of his love." [31]   Genuine
active love of neighbor depends upon a genuine love to
God.   It is not in man's power to say, " I will now love
my neighbor as myself."   To be sure, there is much gracious altruism in the world, for which God is to be de-
voutly thanked, since it is not the altruism of human free
will but that of nature, of maternal and paternal and fra-
ternal, of communal and sexual affection.   But all such
love is afflicted with the vice of partiality.   It has its
foundations, says Edwards,

in the selfish principle. So it is with the natural affection which
parents feel for their children, and with the love which relatives
have one to another. If we except the impulses of instinct, self-
love is the mainspring of it. It is because men love themselves
that they love those persons and things that are their own, or that
they are nearly related to and which they look upon as belonging
to themselves, and which, by the constitution of society, have
their interest and honor linked with their own. . . . There are
many other ways in which self-love is the source of that love and
friendship that often arises between natural men. Most of the
love that there is in the world arises from this principle, and
therefore it does not go beyond nature. And nature cannot go
beyond self-love, but all that men do, is some way or other from
this root.[32]

The extension of self-love, these men might have said,
from the narrow self to the wider self, from the individual
to the family, to the nation, to humanity, to life, still
leaves it attached to its root and so makes it exclusive at
the same time that it seeks to be inclusive.   How can human love be delivered from this partiality and exclusive-

ness and from the consequent tendency to conflict with the excluded reality or from its exploitation? Is not the love of personality, to which intrinsic value is often ascribed, first of all a loyalty to something that is one's own and does it not lead to conflict, since persons are always the greatest foes of persons? Does it not lead also to hatred of the impersonal and to exploitation of nature? The love of life — is it not based on loyalty to that which is primarily our own and does it not lead to that conflict with and to that destruction of life which is ever life's greatest enemy? Does it not also involve the irreverent use of the nonliving as being of purely instrumental value? So also the love of country is the source of conflict with other countries. Patriotism is not enough; neither is the love of persons enough; reverence for life is not enough; love of humanity is not enough. For all such love is self-love though the self be made very large. And the love of self is bad, not because the self is bad but because under the sovereignty of God or in the nature of things it is destructive of other selves and at the same time self-defeating.

There is only one way out of the dilemma of human love. What if men could see that the universal, the eternal, the fountain and center of all being is their true good? What if they could learn to love their neighbors not insofar as these are persons, lives, minds, but because they are creatures of God and sacred by relation to the ultimate Being who is also man's true good? That is precisely the possibility that has been opened in Jesus Christ. In him

the intention of the universe, to speak anthropomorphi-
cally, has become apparent; in his fate, even more than
in his teaching, it has been made manifest that God is
love. Through his life, death and resurrection it has become possible to love the " Enemy " who seemed to destroy all his creatures but now is shown to be seeking their
redemption.

The Awakeners and revivalists led men to the place
whence they could see this God again and see his world
in a new perspective. Hence came that sacramental
sense of all existence which we miscall humanitarianism,
since it was extended to more than human beings and
since its basis was not the goodness of man but the goodness of God. A sacramental sense of nature is expressed
in Edwards' praise of God's wisdom, purity and love appearing " in the sun, moon and stars, in the clouds and
blue sky; in the grass, flowers, trees, in the water and all
nature." [33]   He sees the whole creation as an emanation
of the divine fullness. The sacramental sense of nature
appears particularly in Woolman, who was convinced
that

as the mind was moved by an inward principle to love God as an
invisible, incomprehensible Being, by the same principle it was
moved to love him in all his manifestations in the visible world.
That as by his breath the flame of life was kindled in all animal
and sensible creatures, to say we love God as unseen, and at the
same time exercise cruelty toward the least creature moving by
his life, or by life derived from him, was a contradiction in itself.

.   .   .   .

. . . I looked upon the works of God in this visible creation,
and an awfullness covered me: my heart was tender and often

contrite, and a universal love to my fellow creatures was increased in me. This will be understood by such as have troden in the same path.[34]

John Wesley shows something of this same reverence for life in his sermon, " The General Deliverance," in which he remarks that consideration of the participation of the animals in creation, fall and restoration " may soften our hearts toward the meaner creatures, knowing that the Lord careth for them." [35] Hopkins' principle of universal or disinterested benevolence expresses the same idea in an abstract manner.

Yet it was on the love of man in God that the gospel of the kingdom of Christ put its chief emphasis. God's loyalty to man had been declared most vividly in the life of Christ, and man's apprehension of the excellency of God could bring forth most plentiful fruit in the field of human relations. Not only good men but bad were to be loved; not only their souls but their bodies were to be cherished; not only free men but slaves were to be liberated; and the gospel was to be preached not only to fellow countrymen but also to the inhabitants of strange lands. As the Puritans had insisted that holiness of life does not result from good works, but that where there were no good works it was evident that there was no genuine holiness, so now the revivalists preached in and out of season that works of charity to men could not create love of God, but that true loyalty to God and Christ must show itself in works of active charity to men. The so-called paradox of Calvinism appeared in them again, but after all it was the paradox of Christianity, present quite as much in the

New Testament and in medieval Catholicism as in six-teenth century Protestantism. It is greatly misunder-stood by all those who make the freedom of man their starting point. They say that what was denied on the one hand was affirmed on the other, that the driving force of Calvinism and the Awakening was doubtless due to men's intense desire for heavenly reward or to their fear of hell. The explanation is probably as false psychologically as it is theologically. It would be better to say that the dynamic result of Calvinism as of revival was a validation of the theory which lay back of both. This theory was that human power to do good did not need to be generated but needed only to be released from the bondage to self and the idols, from the conflict in which divided loyalty involved man and in which power inhibited power, from the frustration by which the vanity of all temporal things discouraged life. Deliverance, atonement, hope came from reconciliation to God and from faith in his forgiveness. So when Christians found themselves short of good works, of genuine love to their fellows — as indeed they constantly did — they did not try to whip up their wills by admonitions, threats and promises. They sought to cleanse the fountains of life. In penitence and longing they turned to worship, to self-examination in the presence of God, to the contemplation of the cross of Christ. There were spiritists among them who made worship an escape, there were activists who used worship only as an instrument if at all, and there were sentimentalists who mistook aesthetic or erotic thrills for the love of God.

The essence of the new awakening to the reign of Christ was to be found in none of these, but in faith working by love.

III. THE KINGDOM IN DEED

The revival movement which centered in this gospel produced a manifold activity, as its theory was certain it would do. It was effective moreover far beyond the boundaries of the groups who participated in it directly.

First of all, it resulted in a new tendency toward the withdrawal of the Christian community from entangling alliance with the world and particularly with politics. The movement toward the separation of church and state was supported as actively by most of those who had come under the influence of the revival as it was by Jeffersonian democrats, though both Edwards and Wesley feared separatism almost as much as the Puritans had. In the second place, it organized new orders of Protestant "friars," preachers of the gospel and charitable societies which practiced not so much an intraworldly asceticism as intraworldly loyalty to the kingdom of God. In these new orders and in the older organizations affected by the movement the principle of selected membership was carried through or at least made to modify considerably the lax practices which had come to prevail with respect to membership. It was no more possible now than it had been in the Puritan days to determine with precision who were the truly regenerate, or in whom conviction was thorough and sincere.[36] Men needed to do their best and not set themselves up as the standards. "We do not love the pope," said Whitefield, "because we love to be popes ourselves, and set up our own experience as a standard to others. . . . You may as well say to your neighbor, you have not had a child for you were not in labor all night. The question is whether a child is born; not how long was the preceding pain, but whether it was productive of a new birth, and whether Christ has been formed in your hearts; it is the birth proves the reality of the thing." [37] There were variations and quarrels in the application of the principle of converted membership, but the grand line of the movement was not absolutist. It did not believe that a perfectly pure Christian organization was possible. It did not identify the visible with the invisible church, but it was determined that the visible should try to image the invisible. The result was not only the organization of new societies but the purging of the old churches. Half-Way Covenant and birthright membership needed to give way again in a large part of Congregationalism and Quakerism; "New Side" Presbyterianism sought a converted membership as well as a converted ministry; Baptists with their rejection of the birthright principle began to flourish; Methodist societies with restricted membership and a close-knit discipline began their American career. The object of the movement was not the building of religious institutions; it was really a nondenominational movement; yet the result was a mighty growth in the size and effectiveness of the religious organizations.

The story of the missionary movement which came out of the revival has been frequently told.[38] It is not always recognized that the humanitarian societies of the early nineteenth century were equally closely related to the revival. It fostered the antislavery movement particularly, as the examples of Hopkins, Woolman, Finney and the Methodists indicate. It may be wrong to speak of their movement as antislavery since it was less interested in chastising slaveowners than in freeing slaves and in providing for their education and livelihood. That is one reason why Evangelical groups who were in hearty favor of abolition and who worked for it ardently often found themselves in slight sympathy with the abolitionists. For the latter seemed at times to be more interested in condemning the sin of slaveholders than in promoting the interests of the slaves themselves.[39] Yet one must recognize that at this point Evangelicalism met its greatest defeat despite the noteworthy work done by the Quakers, by the Colonization Society which Hopkins and Alexander sponsored, by the Methodists and Baptists who brought their discipline and preaching to bear upon slaveholders. The freeing of individual slaves and the prohibition of the slave traffic were unable to keep pace with King Cotton's growing demand for serfs. At last the children of the revival needed to go to war, not indeed to free slaves but in an intersectional, political and economic conflict for power. The kingdom of Mars had conquered the kingdom of Christ, and Mars for his own purposes brought liberty to the slaves whom Christ had been unable to free.

Yet this judgment is questionable, for the war-won liberty of the Negro was not liberty indeed and the equality written into laws was neither complete nor practicable in an unconverted kingdom of this world. After war and reconstruction the kingdom of Christ still faced the old task of giving white men freedom from their fetters of pride and race fear, and of granting to black men freedom from the hopelessness and ignorance wherewith they reinforced their masters' bondage. Beyond that the kingdom of Christ faced the additional problem of liberating the new slaves of the northern victors, the growing army in factories and cities of those who, coming from Europe or our own land, became the serfs of a new order of masters.

In other areas the religious enlightenment produced less ambiguous results. Credit must be given to many influences besides the revival for the great development of humanitarian and charitable enterprises which marks the first third of the nineteenth century in America, but it is significant that the leaders of these enterprises were often products of the religious movement. Colleges and secondary schools, which sprang up all over the land like mushrooms after a summer rain, were sponsored in large part by Christian individuals and societies, and in the battle for public schools the revival groups fought on the popular side against institutional churches, who defended their vested interest in education. The Sunday school movement, conceived at first as a humanitarian enterprise, not as an aid to the institutional church, began to flourish. Asylums and societies for the care of the unfortunate, the blind, the deaf and mute, the insane and the feeble-minded, appeared in all parts of the country, and many of them were founded by men and women who had received their inspiration from the religious enlightenment. Every humanitarian cause — temperance, peace, prison reform, the amelioration of poverty — became the rallying point of ardent souls who had been kindled by the gospel of the kingdom of Christ.[40] Yet it was characteristic of the true kingdom that it did not point to these fruits as evidence of its right to exist or defend itself by praising its social utility. For these fruits also Christ not the Christian was to be praised, and God not the church was to be thanked. When all was said and done the Christian knew even better than did his critics how little he had done, how unprofitable was the service he had rendered and how mean was his love compared with the love of Christ.

What was true of the humanitarian enterprises was true also of the cause of political liberty. In some respects the men who had come under the sway of the kingdom of Christ seemed less interested in political liberty than their Puritan ancestors had been. Wesley was a Tory in politics; Jonathan Edwards seems scarcely to have been aware of the political problem. The liberty in which they and their followers were interested was not the liberty defined in the Declaration of Independence. Yet the disciples of the movement were generally to be found on the side of the popular cause against the institutionalists who feared any relaxation of restraint.[41] If they did not share the principles of humanist democrats who believed in the goodness of men neither did they share the prejudices of archconservatives who defended the established order by contending that men were incurably ignorant and vicious.   If they did not become exponents of " Republican Religion " [42] neither did they espouse the static faith in the goodness of existing institutions.   They knew the fallacies present in the dogmas of natural liberty and human goodness, but they also knew that man was not destined to live in ignorance and under restraint. They had confidence in the promise that God would write his laws upon the inward parts and make men fit for liberty, and they knew he was doing it now.   Hence they were not afraid of freedom as the traditionalists were. They did not contend for it save as their contact with the underprivileged made them partisans, or as their opposition to the hopeless reign of restrictive law made them the allies of the humanist democrats, or as their love for the creatures of God bade them seek the equal rights of all. They followed their own line of attack, preaching the kingdom of Christian liberty, the conversion of minds and hearts to the love of God and of man in God.   They pursued the ultimate and permanent revolution, the complete liberty of man in a community of love.   Because they did so the struggles for a limited liberty profited.   In America as in England the Christian enlightenment stood beside the rational enlightenment in the battle for democracy, and it furnished ten soldiers to the cause where the latter furnished one, for it dealt with the common men about whom the rationalists wrote books.

When the final history of America's "golden day" is written it may appear that its brightness was due in no small part to the rule of the kingdom of Christ among freemen who did not use their liberty as an occasion to the flesh but in love served one another. For the extent and meaning of that rule cannot be measured by counting up the number of converts at camp meetings or by psychological analysis of the mass hysterias which were connected with the revival. They can be discovered only if the invisible kingdom, the reign of a spirit and a life communicated and effective in a social body by other means than the very tangible ones, is taken into account.

Such in briefest outline seems to be the story of the great renewal of Christ's kingdom which, not in America alone but in America not least, came upon the land like the sun and rain of spring, refreshing life and promising abundant harvests. It cannot be related as an isolated chapter. Its story stands between the prophet's praise of a sovereign God and the seer's vision of his coming kingdom. Its meaning cannot be retained without ever fresh experience of the life which was manifest in it. But there it stands, a chapter in the past which reaches into the present. In other lands of Christendom it may be possible to ignore the Christian revival of the eighteenth and nineteenth centuries and to seek today the re-establishment of Christianity as it was in or before the Reformation. So the Neo-Protestants of Germany and the Anglocatholics of England believe. For America, however — the land of Edwards, Whitefield, the Tennents, Backus,

Hopkins, Asbury, Alexander, Woolman, Finney and all their company — such an attempt is impossible. It cannot eradicate if it would the marks left upon its social memory, upon its institutions and habits, by an awakening to God that was simultaneous with its awakening to national self-consciousness. It was no wholly new beginning, for the Christianity expressed in it was a more venerable thing than the American nation.[43] Yet for America it was a new beginning; it was our national conversion.

THE COMING KINGDOM

THE CHRISTIAN MOVEMENT in America began with the confession of loyalty to the sovereign God and moved on to experience the reality of the reign of Christ. From the experience it went on to the prayer, " Thy kingdom come; thy will be done on earth as it is in heaven." The three notes of faith in the sovereignty, the experience of the love of Christ and hope of ultimate redemption are inseparable. Divine sovereignty is most patently revealed in such previsions of the coming kingdom as those which the prophets and Jesus made the basis of their proclamation, " Repent for the kingdom of heaven is at hand." For men become aware of the reality and power of the Creator, Judge and Redeemer at the point where human dominion reaches its limits, and these limits are most evident in the end set by death or social catastrophe. In this way awareness of the coming kingdom is as much the presupposition as it is the consequence of faith in God's sovereignty. The reign of Christ also finds its fulfillment and its meaning in the manifestation of divine justice and love at the end of all things. To live under that reign is to say with Paul: " Ourselves also, who have the first fruits of the Spirit, even we ourselves groan within ourselves, waiting for the adoption, to wit, the redemption of our body. For we are saved by hope." The theological definition of the relation of these three elements in the Christian life is as difficult as the definition of the Trinity. Our concern, however, is not with definition of abstract ideas so much as with description of the relation as it appears in the limited area of American Christianity. And it is evident that the story of faith in the kingdom of God cannot be told without reference to the hope of its manifestation in power. For this hope was implicit in the period which emphasized sovereignty, became more explicit as the idea of Christ's reign prevailed, and appeared as the leading element in the faith of the nineteenth century. The nature of this hope, its development and its relation to the ideas of sovereignty and salvation must be the subject of our further inquiry.

I. The Beginning of Hope

The strain toward the kingdom's coming upon earth was not strong in the earliest period of Protestant Christianity. Upon the whole, it seems, the Puritans had not as yet brought their hope of the future into line with their fundamental faith in the living sovereignty of God. They still defined it in terms of the orthodox Western belief which had issued out of the combination of a Greek vision of the eternal with the Hebrew expectation of world renewal by the power of God. In that synthetic hope the emphasis lay upon Greek elements. The goal of life was eternity rather than a new time, immortality of the spirit rather than resurrection of the body. The dividing line between time and eternity was most discernible at the point of death, which was the crisis through which the soul needed to pass. Though the Hebrew hope was recognized in the doctrines of last judgment and general resurrection, Christian interest centered in the heaven into which souls entered one by one. Such books as Baxter's *Saints' Everlasting Rest*, and Bunyan's *Pilgrim's Progress*, and the Anglican Taylor's *Holy Living* and *Holy Dying* — all of them widely used in America — expressed this tension toward the future and the Christian's anticipations. The same interest prevailed in the devotional books of Roger Williams and of Thomas Shepard.

This setting of the affections upon the eternal was of great importance in guiding men in their work of construction. It meant for them that they did not confuse the present order of grace with the order of glory and that they could organize their mundane life by means of institutions whose preparatory and finite character was recognized. Like Williams they could look upon the political and social movements in which they took leading parts with the detachment of those who do not belong to this world, where " vanity and vexation " abound. Their citizenship was in another country of tranquillity and peace. At the same time they needed to regard the mundane life with a strong sense of responsibility, for they understood that temporal affairs needed to be managed so that things eternal would not be lost. It is a mistake to regard the individualistic vision of the end and the indi-

vidualistic hope as detrimental to the sense of social responsibility. This had not been true of a Plato whose
highly spiritual doctrine of last things was mated with the
projection of a republic designed to mediate the eternal to
man; neither had it been true of medieval monks; it was
not true now of Protestants. Yet it does appear that
under the influence of the hope of individual salvation society was conceived in rather static terms — as an affair of
institutions and laws rather than as a common life with a
grand destiny comparable to that of the human soul. Insofar as the coming kingdom was regarded as wholly spiritual it remained distinct from that faith in living sovereignty which formed the basis of Protestant construction.
While the sovereign God ruled the whole of life, the coming kingdom was for the soul alone.

Though the individualistic and spiritualistic view of
the world beyond prevailed among Puritans, the social,
temporalistic idea of divine judgment and salvation was
inescapable for men who regarded the Hebrew Scriptures
as the record of divine revelation. In contrast to the philosopher the Hebrew prophet saw the relativity of human
dominion and the reality of the divine kingdom made
manifest in the crises of social rather than of individual
life. Not the death of the body but the doom which
threatened societies revealed the sovereignty of God.
The promise appeared not in the immortal character of
the soul but in the hope of the resurgence and transformation of the social life. The kingdom of prophetic vision
was moreover a coming kingdom, not one which lay be-

yond a vale of tears. Men were hastening toward it, but it was hastening toward them with even greater urgency. "Thou dost not hasten more than the Most High," God had said, "for thy haste is for thine own self, but he that is above hasteneth on behalf of many." [1] The idea of the coming kingdom was intimately connected, in other words, with the faith in the living initiative of God. None of the Puritans could entirely escape the influence of this conception and for some of them it came to be of central importance. The more the idea of the end and goal of life was brought into relation to their fundamental faith in sovereignty, the more it came to be an idea of the coming kingdom rather than of the other world. To so Hebraic a man as Eliot and to the somewhat less Hebraic Hooker the political upheavals of the day brought home the crisis of human life, the divine aggression and the opportunity for a salvation which was not for the soul alone.

The preface to Eliot's *Christian Commonwealth, or The Civil Policy of the Rising Kingdom of Jesus Christ* shows how he interpreted the English crisis of civil war and Commonwealth days in terms of the coming kingdom. "Christ is coming to set up his Kingdom," he believed, though "the coming of Christ is in Clouds of darkness," so that many fail to be persuaded of his advent.

Christ is the only right Heir of the Crown of England, and of all other Nations; and he is now come to take possession of his Kingdom, making England first in that blessed work of setting up the Kingdom of the Lord Jesus: and in order thereunto, he hath cast down not only the miry Religion, but also the former form of civil Government, which did stick so fast unto it, until by an unavoidable necessity, it fell with it; which while it stood, and as it stood, was too high to stoop to the Lord Jesus, to be ruled by his command.[2]

Thomas Hooker also considers the crises of the day in the light of the promise. Christ has taken back to himself, he believes, the priestly and prophetic offices and is about to assume kingly power. " These are the times drawing on, wherein Prophecies are to attain their performances. . . . This being the season, when all the kingdomes of the world, are becoming the Lords and his Christs: and to this purpose he is taking to himself his great might which heretofore he seemed to lay aside and in silence." [3] This mood of expectancy was chastened by the reflection that the end was not yet at hand and that though the " present term of Gods patience promiseth some allowance to his people," it did not permit the full liberty of the order of glory. Hugh Peters and Sir Henry Vane, who returned to England to participate in the great struggles of the mother country, seem to have shared the apocalyptic spirit of an Eliot.[4]

Among the Quakers the tension toward the coming kingdom of God was more pronounced. The symbol of divine judgment for them was not so much death as social catastrophe or decay. The spires of Lichfield cathedral which struck at Fox's life bore witness to the bloodguiltiness of the church and the town. It is the old prophetic vision of the end which causes him to cry, " Woe to the bloody city! " and makes him see " a channel of blood running down the streets and the market place like a pool of blood." [5]   How apocalyptic is the great cry to Friends in the ministry:

Sound, sound ye faithful servants of the Lord, and witnesses in his name, . . . and prophets of the Highest, and angels of the Lord! Sound ye all abroad in the world, to the awakening and raising of the dead, that they may be awakened and raised up out of the grave, to hear the voice that is living. . . . Sound, sound the pleasant and melodious sound; sound, sound ye trumpets, the melodious sound abroad, that all the deaf ears may be opened to hear the pleasant sound of the trumpet to judgment and life, to condemnation and light.[6]

Apocalyptic also is Dewsbury's address to the " people . . . scattered into Barbados, Virginia, New England and other islands thereaways and countries elsewhere," wherein he announces that " the mighty Day of the Lord is coming, and in His power is appearing amongst you." [7] The Quaker itinerants in England and the New World lived in the last days of a social order as philosophers and monks lived in the presence of death.   They saw the kingdom of God coming in power.

The Quaker's hope of the coming kingdom distinguished itself from that of the radical millenarians, represented in England by the Fifth Monarchy men and in America less radically by John Eliot, by being intimately associated with the experience of the kingdom of Christ. The coming kingdom in their conception was not only a manifestation of divine majesty and the apocalypse of human sin, it was even more the reign of love.   They were unable to follow in the path of violent revolutionaries who felt themselves called upon to execute divine justice; they believed that the promise of the coming kingdom could be realized only by those who accepted judgment with the meekness and humility of Christ and entered into the life of joy without swords in their hands. This necessary approximation of the coming kingdom to the kingdom of Christ led them, however, into a new difficulty. They were inclined to bring the future revolution into the present and to say that the kingdom had come to those of whom the spirit of Christ had taken possession. For such the crisis was past; the revolution was over; the coming kingdom had become a present one. Hence the Quaker was a perfectionist in his social and individual ethics, for he now lived in the new world of God; the interim which had justified a relative ethics of the restraint of evil was over.

Yet he discovered in practice that the kingdom of Christ was by no means the coming kingdom. In fact, if not in theory, he lived in an interim in which he needed to make constant adjustments to an unredeemed world and to abandon his perfectionism. He provided for police power for the restraint of evil; he voted monies for the defense of his state, though he sought to ease his conscience by calling gunpowder grain and by allowing the non-Quaker executive to bear the onus of engaging in unchristian conduct in the military defense of the state. When compromises became too difficult he was required to recognize the incompleteness of the Christian revolution by abandoning either his Quakerism or the responsibility for public office. In fact he lived between two revolutions, and the effort to identify the second with the first ended with the actual recognition that though God ruled and though his rule was partly realized in the kingdom of Christ, yet his kingdom had not yet come in power and glory to deliver men from their rebellion, fear and violence.[8]

At the end of the period of settlement the tension of men toward the coming kingdom slackened. As the sovereignty of God became the rule of an absentee monarch, as the kingdom of Christ became a religious institution, so the coming kingdom, insofar as it was judgment, became a familiar and unreal crisis; insofar as it was promise it came to be either a fairly certain future prosperity and peace or an equally comfortable heaven to which souls were admitted by an indulgent God on recommendation of his kindly son. The main question was one of early reservations. The prudent sought to make sure in ample time of advantageous positions for the seeing of celestial visions and the hearing of angelic choirs. The happily imprudent were ready to take a chance on the cancelled reservations of the saints.

II. The Growth of Hope

The Great Awakening and the revivals were ushered in by a new awareness of the coming kingdom. Edwards and Wesley, like Paul and Luther before them, became intensely conscious of the great gap which exists between human performance and divine demand or between the actuality and the potentiality of human life. They saw a great opportunity and they strained all their efforts toward its realization. Like the earnest Wesleys in the days of the Holy Club, Edwards determined with youthful enthusiasm and self-confidence to seek " as much happiness, in the other world, as I possibly can, with all the power, might, vigour, and vehemence, yea violence, I am capable of, or can bring myself to exert, in any way that can be thought of." [9] He adopted, reaffirmed and revised his resolutions; he disciplined himself; he seemed to be ever more careful to discover all the means possible for advancing his soul toward the great future happiness. No medieval monk or seeker of utopia kept the goal more constantly before his eyes or sought to advance toward it more strenuously than did this Protestant monastic. The other leaders seem to have followed the same general pattern. [10] Their hope was like that of their contemporaries; it was still the orthodox Western expectation of life in heaven. But they differed from others in the intensity of their anticipation. What to most men was an extra consolation and a supernatural addition to their expectations of success and joy on earth was very close, real and important to the embryonic Evangelicals. They felt keenly the wonder and the nearness of this possibility of life and, by the same token, the unsatisfactoriness of their present existence. They pressed therefore into the kingdom of God, as they understood that kingdom.

Their efforts failed — or, we may say, they were crowned

with success as a result of failure. It became clear to them that though it was not possible for men to make the potential actual, yet what was impossible for men was both possible and actual for God. The idea of the coming kingdom came alive when it was connected with the conviction of God's living power. As the moralism of the Holy Club was supplanted by the gospel of salvation so the Edwardean effort to progress toward the coming kingdom by self-discipline gave way to the recognition of divine sovereignty. Under these circumstances anticipations of the future became more rather than less intense. Now the coming kingdom appeared not as a goal toward which men were traveling but as the end which was hastening toward them; and now it was no longer simply the great happiness which men might miss but also the great threat which they could not escape. The new note was related to the old in the same way that communism in our time is related to utopian socialism.

The " hell-fire " sermons, which often seemed to be the only part of Edwards' preaching that later generations remembered, are profoundly misunderstood when they are taken out of their context in the theology of divine sovereignty and placed in the context of an institutionalism which used threats of hell like promises of heaven to frighten or to wheedle the immature into obedient acceptance of conventional piety and morality. Placed in their proper setting they represent Edwards' intense awareness of the precariousness of life's poise, of the utter insecurity of men and of mankind which are at every moment as ready to plunge into the abyss of disintegration, barbarism, crime and the war of all against all, as to advance toward harmony and integration. He recognized what Kierkegaard meant when he described life as treading water with ten thousand fathoms beneath us.[11]

Man is preserved in his precarious balance, according to Edwards, only by the patience of God, in whose eyes the spawning, lusting, fighting, cruel life of humanity could scarcely be more lovely than insect existence is to men. " The God that holds you over the pit of hell, much as one holds a spider, or some loathsome insect over the fire, abhorrs you and is dreadfully provoked: his wrath toward you burns like fire, . . . he is of purer eyes than to bear to have you in his sight. . . . It is nothing but his hand that holds you from falling into the fire every moment." [12]

What the prophets had realized was understood again by Edwards and his co-laborers: " Woe to you that desire the day of the Lord. The day of the Lord is darkness and not light." The coming kingdom understood as the apocalypse of the divine sovereignty was the fruition not only of divine goodness but of human badness in conflict with that unconquerable goodness. How much the Awakeners and revivers realized that the coming kingdom meant crisis as well as promise is evident from the titles of some of their sermons. Edwards preached not only on " Sinners in the Hand of an Angry God " but also on " Future Punishment of the Wicked Unavoidable and Intolerable," " The Eternity of Hell Torments," "The Final Judgment," "The Wicked Useful in their Destruction Only," "Wrath Upon the Wicked to the Uttermost," "The End of the Wicked Contemplated by the Righteous." To these titles one may add Whitefield's "The Eternity of Hell Torments," Wesley's "The Great Assize," "The Signs of the Times," "Of Hell," "On Redeeming the Times" and many more similar subjects by their followers. As for John the Baptist and the Jesus of the Synoptic Gospels, the dramatic crisis of the impending future revealed to the American disciples the actual crisis in the present. To be sure the Evangelicals dealt with individual men who thought themselves secure in their isolation; they thought of the crisis in which the individual stood and used death as the symbol in which the threat to security became apparent, whereas the prophets of the Old and New Testaments saw the crisis under the symbol of social catastrophe. But in addressing individuals the Awakeners dealt as faithfully with their own time as the prophets had done with theirs. For judgment and death and the peril of falling into a state of worthless existence belong to all things human.

The recognition that the coming kingdom of the divine sovereign meant destruction of much that men prized and that it called for their immediate turning away from the ways that led to darkness was only half of the Awakeners' gospel. The second element was good news. Beyond judgment lay the new world of God, the kingdom of joy and peace, of unity and harmony, the realization of all the good potential in that human life in which so much evil was also potential. The good news was not only that there was light beyond darkness, but even more that in Christ men had been given the opportunity to anticipate both threat and promise, to bring the future into the present and to receive a foretaste of the coming kingdom, a validation of the promise. John Woolman offers as excellent an illustration of the way in which the eighteenth century could anticipate the coming kingdom as Paul does of the first century. He wrote in his *Journal;*

> In a time of Sickness with plurisie a little upward of two years and a half ago I was brought so Near the gates of death, that I forgot my name. Being then desirous to know who I was, I saw a mass of matter of a dull gloomy collour, between the South and the East, and was informed that this mass was human beings, in as great misery as they could be, & live, and that I was mixed in with them, & henceforth I might not consider myself as a distinct or Separate being. In this state I remained several hours. I then heard a soft melodious voice, more pure and harmonious than any voice I had heard with my ears before, and I believe it was the voice of an angel who spake to the other angels. The words were John Woolman is dead. I soon remembered that I once was John Woolman, and being assured that I was alive in the body, I greatly wondered what that heavenly voice could mean.

When " the mystery was opened " he " perceived there was Joy in heaven over a Sinner who had repented, and that that language, *John Woolman is dead,* meant no more than the death of my own will." [13] The experiences of the thousands who met the crisis of life under the influences of Quaker and Evangelical preaching were doubtless usually less visionary, less complete and often less sincere. There are few Woolmans and Edwards' in any generation. Still, many experiences were genuine and through them American Christians in the eighteenth and early nineteenth centuries anticipated the coming kingdom by dying to self and rising with Christ.

The reality and the surprising scope of these experiences now brought a great surmise and hope to the leaders. What if this movement were itself the coming of the kingdom in power? It is remarkable how under the influence of the Great Awakening the millenarian expectation flourished in America. Hopkins remarks that few writers in the seventeenth century said anything about this doctrine but " in the present century there has been more attention to it." [14] To Edwards the surprising conversions indicated that " it is not unlikely that this work of God's Spirit, so extraordinary and wonderful, is the dawning, or at least a prelude of that glorious work of God, so often foretold in Scripture, which, in the progress and issue of it, shall renew the world of mankind." He gave various reasons why " we cannot reasonably think otherwise, than that the beginning of this great work of God must be near. And there are many things that make it probable that this work will begin in America." [15] The Awakening appeared to him to be

a great and wonderful event, a strange revolution, an unexpected surprising overturning of things, suddenly brought to pass. . . . It is the work of redemption (the great end of all the other works

of God, and of which the work of creation was but a shadow)
in the event, success, and end of it: It is the work of new creation
which is infinitely more glorious than the old. . . . The New
Jerusalem in this respect has begun to come down from heaven,
and perhaps never were more of the prelibations of heaven's
glory given upon earth.[16]

In the *History of the Work of Redemption* and *An
Humble Attempt to Promote Explicit Agreement and
Visible Union of God's People in Extraordinary Prayers
for the Revival of Religion* this millennial idea is developed. How the future revolution has been anticipated
and the time foreshortened appears in this statement
from the former work:

The end of God's creating the world, was to prepare a kingdom for his Son . . . which should remain to all eternity. So
far as the *kingdom of Christ is set* up in the world, so far is the
world brought to its end, and the eternal state of things set up —
so far are all the great changes and revolutions in the world
brought to their everlasting issue, and all things come to their
ultimate period. . . . So far as Christ's kingdom is established
in the world, so far are things wound up and settled in their everlasting state, and a period put to the course of things in this
changeable world, so far are the first heavens and the first earth
come to an end, and the new heavens and the new earth, the
everlasting heavens and earth established in their room.[17]

Edwards believed that this *so far* must fall short of perfection and, following the Scriptures, he predicted a time
of great wickedness in a world which had been made
populous and prosperous as a result of its acceptance of
the reign of Christ. Beyond the millennium then stood

the last crisis and final revolution.[18] Yet it is remarkable how his interest had shifted from the eternal kingdom into which souls enter one by one to the kingdom coming upon earth. He did not abandon the double doctrine of the future, but as he became more convinced of the power of God and of the reality of the Christian revolution the idea of the kingdom's coming to earth took a certain precedence. God had made possible what was impossible for men.

Many efforts have been made to account for the prevalence in American Christianity of the millenarian tendency. It has been erroneously ascribed to the early Calvinists and with greater reason to the left-wing Protestants. Yet the Awakening and the revivals seem above all to have made it the common and vital possession of American Christians. They brought the remote possibility very near. The rise in American faith of the idea of the coming kingdom was not due to an importation from the outside, that is, from rationalism or political idealism. It arose out of the Christian movement which had begun with the conviction of divine sovereignty, been led thence to the realization of Christ's kingdom and now saw clearly that the latter led toward the realization of man's everlasting hope.

Edwards was not the only one in whom this development came to light. Samuel Hopkins was another millenarian. Channing says of him: " The millennium was his chosen ground. If any subject of thought possessed him above all others, I suppose it to have been this. The millennium was more than a belief to him. It had the freshness of visible things. He was at home in it. . . . Whilst to the multitude he seemed a hard, dry theologian, feeding on the thorns of controversy, he was living in a region of imagination, feeding on visions of a holiness and happiness which are to make earth all but heaven." [19] His millenarianism like Edwards' was based upon faith in divine sovereignty and the experience of the order of grace. Neither of these men thought of the coming kingdom in terms of supernatural appearances, save as the work of awakening, of regeneration and of the reconciliation of man to God could be regarded as supernatural. They did not engage in the mathematical calculations and astrological speculations of the literalists. The millennium was the reign of Christ; the reign of Christ was one of love to God, and therefore to man; and love came through the " cleansing of the inward parts." " By the new heaven and new earth is meant," Hopkins wrote, " the work of redemption, or the church redeemed by Christ. . . . To suppose that Christ shall come in his human nature to this earth, and live here in his whole person visibly, a thousand years, before the day of judgment," appears to be contrary to Scripture and it is contrary to reason as well.[20]

Though the instruments of the reign of Christ were spiritual its sphere was this world. Edwards and Hopkins had no intention of saying to men that the fruits of the spirit were purely spiritual, invisible to the eye. They insisted on the visibility of Christ's rule in the social as well as in the personal sphere. The time of the kingdom of heaven on earth, said Edwards, will be " a time of great light and *knowledge* " especially in the doctrines of religion; " it shall be a time of great *holiness;* . . . religion shall in every respect be *uppermost* in the world." But it will also be a time of " universal peace and a good understanding among the nations of the world; . . . it will be a time of *excellent order* in the church of Christ," which is to be beautiful and glorious, and it " will be a time of the greatest *temporal prosperity* " as well as of rejoicing. For " such a spiritual estate as we have just described, has a natural tendency to health and long life, . . . to procure ease, quietness, pleasantness, and cheerfulness of mind, also wealth and a great increase of children," to which he adds that " temporal prosperity will also be promoted by a remarkable blessing from heaven." [21]

Hopkins prophesied that the millennium resulting from Christ's coming in the hearts would be a time of eminent holiness or of disinterested love to God and man. While he also emphasized the increase of religious knowledge he added that men will have " sufficient leisure to pursue and acquire learning of every kind that will be beneficial to themselves and to society; . . . great advances will be made in all arts and sciences and in every useful branch of knowledge, which tends to promote the spiritual and eternal good of men, or their convenience and comfort in this life." It is, furthermore, to be a time of universal peace, love, and general and cordial friendship; religious unity will accompany political peace; it will be a " time of great enjoyment, happiness and universal joy " for spiritual but also for material reasons. Natural calamities will be prevented by divine providence; war with its impoverishment of men will have been abolished; intemperance and excess will be discarded; " the art of husbandry will be greatly advanced, and men will have skill to cultivate and manure the earth in a much better and easy way than ever before "; there will be " great improvement in the mechanic arts by which the earth will be subdued and cultivated, and all the necessary and convenient articles of life, such as utensils, clothing, buildings, etc. will be formed and made in a better manner, and with much less labor than they now are "; finally, " there will then be such benevolence and fervent charity . . . that all worldly things will be in a great degree and in the best manner common, so as not to be withheld from any who may want them." [22]

Wesley, who although he was an Englishman was yet the most influential Methodist in America, offers us a further example of this millenarianism. He also foreshortened the future and brought the great revolution into the present, though it may be with more caution than the New Englanders displayed. He said:

I cannot induce myself to think that God has wrought so glorious a work, to let it sink and die away in a few years: no, I trust, this is only the beginning of a far greater work; the " dawn of the *latter day glory*." . . . Before the end even the rich shall enter into the kingdom of God. Together with them will enter in the great, the noble, the honourable; yea, the rulers, the princes, the kings of the earth. Last of all, the wise, the learned, the men of genius, the philosophers, will be convinced that they are fools; will be " converted and become as little children " and " enter into the kingdom of God." . . . All unprejudiced persons may see with their eyes, that [God] is already renewing the face of the earth and we have strong reason to hope that the work he has begun, he will carry on to the day of the Lord Jesus.[23]

He sounds a characteristic note, also, when he explains that he does not himself affirm Bengel's thought that the millennium would begin in 1836. " I do not determine any of these things: they are too high for me. I only desire to creep on in the vale of humble love." [24] Wesley was cautious in every way, yet he expected great things — the dawn of the day of glory.

The Quakers, as we have seen, had from the beginning anticipated the coming revolution and brought it into the present in the spiritual coming of Christ. Their millenarianism in the time of the Awakening and the revivals was somewhat less enthusiastic than that of Edwards and Hopkins. Perhaps their longer experience had taught them to be cautious. The revolution Woolman looked for was an individual event taking place in human souls. But the results which he expected were social — the freeing of slaves, the reduction of economic desire, the elimination of poverty through the decrease of wealth which requires poverty for its support, the cessation of war and the establishment of harmony among men.[25]

Summarizing the development of the Evangelical expectation of the coming kingdom we may say that it was based solidly on the ideas of divine sovereignty and of the crisis in which this sovereignty involved sinful men; its second foundation was the idea of the kingdom of Christ, without which the coming kingdom was darkness and not light. The Awakening and the revivals tended to bring the coming kingdom into the present and to insist that the spiritual revolution could be and needed to be faced now. Then, as the success of this gospel became manifest, a great wave of expectancy came over men. The kingdom of God on earth had come very near, not as a result of moralistic endeavors after perfection but in consequence of the power of the gospel of reconciliation. It had come near through the miracle of mass conversion and through the validation of the promise that to those who sought first the kingdom and its righteousness all other things would be added.[26] A Christian revolution was evidently taking place; a new day was dawning. In one sense of the word this gospel of the coming kingdom which had begun with men in their solitariness became definitely social, for it had social effects in mind. It insisted that the fruits of the personal revolution needed to appear and, insofar as the revolution was genuine, would appear in the whole common life, in science, art, agriculture, industry, church and state. There were variations among the leaders on many minor issues but on two major points they were in fundamental agreement. In the first place they knew that the promise could not be divorced from the crisis, or that there was no way into the kingdom of God on earth which did not pass through the darkness of loss and the death to the self. In the second place they agreed on the necessity of meeting the future crisis so far as possible in the present, of pressing into the kingdom which was coming inevitably with its judgment and its promise.[27]

There was a third point of agreement, though the assent to it was one of common silence. The way into the coming kingdom lay, these men all believed, through the kingdom of Christ; the function of the church was to prepare men for crisis and for promise by proclaiming to them the gospel of repentance and faith rather than by persuading them to undertake specific political activity.[28] It is a constant source of astonishment to many modern interpreters of the Evangelical movement that its leaders paid so little attention to politics. Edwards, as we have seen, was silent on the subject. Wesley and his followers were proud of the fact that politics were never mentioned in Methodist pulpits. Hopkins' mind was not on American independence, grateful as he was for it, but rather on the fact that the colonies could expect no deliverance out of their calamities or success of their warfare unless they repented of the sin of slavery and made all restitution in their power to its victims.[29] Though Finney, in the later time, was one of the chief inspirers of the antislavery movement he wrote his memoirs without referring to the Civil War. These astonishing silences were not due to indifference, as the last two examples show especially, but rather to the fact that such men regarded Revolution and

Civil War as civil conflicts which would not settle the issue of the future. They did not say, as their successors might, that such conflicts settle no question save the one of balance of power, but by their relative indifference toward them they showed that they had little faith in progress toward a true peace by any means save those of the Christian revolution. At the same time their confidence in the gospel was so great that they were not tempted to attach it to the chariots of secular parties. They represented again the spirit of those Old Testament loyalists of the kingdom who did not care greatly whether their nation remained politically independent or became powerful, but who wept over the unrighteousness of their people and died storming the ramparts of internal injustice.

III. " The Golden Day "

The expectation of the coming kingdom upon earth which the Quakers had brought with them and the Great Awakening had made vivid was nurtured by the continuing revival until it became the dominant idea in American Christianity. If the seventeenth was the century of the sovereignty and the eighteenth the time of the kingdom of Christ, the nineteenth may be called the period of the coming kingdom. The great hopefulness which prevailed in all areas of life in the time from the Revolution to the World War was due to many factors besides the experience of the Christian movement, but it is likely that the latter was one of its major sources.[30] Among the

Christians of America, at least, the optimism of the nine-teenth century was intimately connected with the expe-rience of the anticipated Christian revolution.

The hope of the kingdom-to-come was subject to many exaggerations and perversions during this period. It was secularized by being detached from its context of faith in the sovereignty and of the experience of grace, while it was attached to the ideas of human sovereignty and natu-ral freedom. It was nationalized, being used to support the feeling of national superiority and of manifest des-tiny. It was confused with the progress of industrialism and capitalism. It was conceived in tragically literal fash-ion by the Millerites.[31] It was used to justify war and vio-lence as in the days of the English crisis. But even these abnormal forms of the hope indicated the power it had over the minds of American Christians. To an ever in-creasing extent they turned from the expectation of heav-enly bliss to the hope of a radical transformation of life upon earth, without abandoning the former as though the two expectations were exclusive of each other.

Many interpreters of the so-called " social gospel " have assumed that prior to 1907 or 1890 the hope of a kingdom on earth was practically nonexistent while Chris-tians directed all their expectations to the heavenly city. Not only Edwards and Hopkins but many of their fol-lowers in the succeeding decades appear as witnesses to dispute the correctness of this conception. We must not look primarily to New England for the later witnesses, since the Christian movement there entered into one of those periods of institutionalization which frequently follow a time of energetic activity. Nathanael W. Taylor was spokesman for the prevailing view when he emphasized the transitoriness of this world and directed the minds of his hearers toward the everlasting glory beyond.[32] The vision of God rather than his kingdom was the attraction. Yet Lyman Beecher testified to the presence of some millennial spirit among the Congregationalists. Of his many utterances on the subject the following extract from a missionary sermon is typical: " What the mind and counsel of God have purposed to do for the melioration of man is now hastening to its consummation with the intenseness of infinite benevolence, under the guidance of unerring wisdom and by the impulse of Almighty Power. . . . The lines are now drawing, and preparation is fast making for the battle of the great day of God Almighty." [33]   Equally typical however is the fact that his next appeal is to the hope of heaven.

The dynamic movement of the time in New England inclined toward a humanism which separated it from the main line of the Christian movement. In it the hope of the kingdom was detached from the ideas of sovereignty and redemption. Yet of William Ellery Channing this is not wholly true and he may legitimately be counted among the heirs of the Evangelical movement. He owed more to the Awakeners than he was aware, and his humanitarianism and disinterested love of God were akin in many ways to those of the theocratic Hopkins.[34]   He gloried in the " privilege of existing in a universe of progressive order and beauty," [35] and turned ever more from the interest in moral self-culture to the realization of love and justice in social relations. His ultimate hope, to be sure, remained primarily spiritual and individualistic.[36] Yet he saw in the victory of Christ's spirit the coming of his kingdom to earth.

> The Christian, whose inward eyes and ears are touched by God, [he wrote] discerns the coming of Christ, hears the sound of his chariot wheels and the voice of his trumpet, when no other perceives them. He discerns the Saviour's advent in the dawning of higher truth on the world, in new aspirations of the church after perfection, in the prostration of prejudice and error, in brighter expressions of Christian love, in more enlightened and intense consecration of the Christian to the cause of humanity, freedom and religion. Christ comes in the conversion, the regeneration, the emancipation of the world.[37]

Concretely Christ's spirit demands the abolition of war and slavery, the practice of philanthropy and the government of all life by reference to the dignity and worth of men.

As Channing's example indicates, the hope of the coming kingdom was closely bound up with the evangelistic and humanitarian enterprises which grew and blossomed in connection with the revival movement. To many of the men who participated in them or observed them these were evidences of its coming and at the same time instruments whereby the kingdom was being hastened. The missionary movement seemed even to the most restrained among its interpreters the sign that God was preparing a great revolution.[38]   When Mark Hopkins looked back in 1850 upon a half century of reform movements and of social progress he saw in them evidences of the consummation of God's plan — the subjugation of the world by Christianity, a triumph which involved the perfection of society.   Prior to 1800, he wrote, Christianity had " practically fallen back from her undertaking, not knowing the extent or character of her field."   But at about the commencement of the new century " the command of Christ, interpreted by modern discoveries, began to work in the heart of the church."   And so, with Christianity as the fundamental force though not the only agency, and as the terminus, the ocean of all the rivers of reform, a new prospect is opening before men, a nobler end than had before been conceived.[39]

Among the Presbyterians the influence of the revivals on the one hand and that of Thomas Chalmers on the other modified a conservative tendency toward other-worldliness and encouraged expectations of an earthly approximation of the heavenly kingdom.[40]

In the groups most directly affected by the revival the millennial hope is strongest.   Alexander Campbell names his magazine *The Millenial Harbinger* and announces in its first number that " this work shall have for its object the developement and introduction of that political and religious order of society called the Millenium, which will be the consummation of that ultimate amelioration of society proposed in the Christian Scriptures."   Among the measures which are to be fostered in pursuit of the high goal he lists not only the destruction of sectarianism but the extension of public education in order that men may be prepared for rational and social happiness, the elimination of injustices that remain in political regulations and the emancipation of the African slaves. There is no fixing of bounds, he believes, " to the maximum of social and refined bliss which would flow from the very general or universal prevalence and triumphs of Evangelical principles." [41] The temper of the Campbellite movement is expressed moreover in a circular letter which declares that " the Christian of the nineteenth century has been stationed by Providence on a sublime eminence, from which he can behold the fulfillment of illustrious prophecies and look backwards upon nearly the whole train of events leading to the millennium." [42] Two interests of the later social gospel are manifest in these pronouncements; on the one hand attention is directed to the attainment of happiness in a mundane social order; upon the other hand the call is for an active or " muscular " Christianity. " Practical men," says Campbell, " have always been the most useful; and, therefore, practical principles have been more beneficial to mankind than the most ingenious and refined speculations."

Finney enunciates the hope of the coming kingdom clearly and gives a good account of its relation to the experience of conversion. In this follower of Edwards and Hopkins the faith in divine sovereignty, now expressed in terms of moral government, together with the recognition of depravity supplies the foundation for the

central Christian experience of regeneration, the " radical
change of the ultimate intention, end or object of life,"
the turning from self as the end to " God and the interests
of his kingdom." [43]   Such a change must result in and be
evidenced by disinterested benevolence.   Finney insists
once more with Protestant and Evangelistic vehemence
upon the " now."   Now was the time for gaining assurance of salvation; the great revolution might be anticipated now.   All the attacks on his views of sanctification
center on this point.   He believes, with his predecessors,
that insofar as men were reconciled to God's will his kingdom had come, and insofar as men were converted from
self to God and his interests they brought forth fruits of
righteousness in actual social life.   " As they supremely
value the highest good of being, they will and must take
a deep interest in whatever is promotive of that end.
Hence their spirit is necessarily that of the reformer.   For
the universal reformation of the world they stand committed. . . . For this end they live and have their being.
. . . They are predisposed to lay hold on whatever gives
promise of good to man."   It is " their business, their profession, their life " to promote reform.   " The cause of
peace, the cause of antislavery, and that of the overthrow
of licentiousness must lie near the heart of every truly
benevolent mind."   From the beginning the business of
the saints has been the introduction of the gospel as divine
revelation, the organization " of the visible kingdom of
God on earth," the laying of foundations for universal reform.[44]   Finney's emphasis lies on the kingdom of Christ

rather than on the coming kingdom, but he had seen the close relation between the two and his work everywhere led to endeavors after the reformation of social life.

Under his influence, but also for other reasons, the interest of the party of the kingdom of God was concentrated during the second third of the nineteenth century in the antislavery movement. How much millennial spirit there was in this movement appears in the activity of Theodore Weld, Finney's disciple and an antislavery leader. The days of slavery are numbered, he is certain, " in this land of liberty, and light, and revivals of millennial glory." Even a slight success in the movement prompts him to jubilate: " If these are the *first* fruits, what will be the *Harvest?* . . . If the gathering of handfuls wakes up such loud acclaim, what will be the song when the morning stars break out together, . . . as the whole mighty growth that now stands as a forest, and shakes like Lebanon, comes before the Lord of the harvest, and is gathered into his garner? " [45] There is manifest in Weld the spirit which makes Edward Beecher cry in 1865, " Now that God has smitten slavery unto death, he has opened the way for the redemption and sanctification of our whole social system." [46]

Weld regards the revivals, moral reform, temperance, women's rights and antislavery movements as parts of one whole. " Let Delavan drive temperance, McDowell moral reform, Finney revivals, Tappan antislavery, etc. Each of these is bound to make his own *peculiar* department his *main* business, and to promote *collaterally* as much as he can the other objects. I have no doubt but Finney has erred in not giving as much *collateral* attention to antislavery as the present emergent crisis demands." [47]   Finney sees it in a somewhat different light. These movements are connected, yet one among them, the revival, must take precedence if they are not all to come to grief. To him such abolitionists as H. B. Stanton show the spirit and the language of the slave driver and he sees clearly that a moralism which seeks the kingdom on earth by means other than repentance and faith is driving the church and the world, ecclesiastical and state leaders, into " one common infernal squabble that will roll a wave of blood over the land." Only by making abolition an appendage, as he says, of the revival of religion can the country be saved, or the liberty and soul of the slave.[48] Finney stands for the old principle; the hope of the coming of the kingdom to earth is based on the experience of the kingdom of Christ; Weld partly agrees with him, but Tappan and many another reformer think Finney a coward because he seeks abolition by regeneration rather than by fighting.

One other point regarding the coming kingdom as seen in connection with the antislavery movement needs to be noted. No small portion of the energy developed by that movement came from the realization that the coming kingdom was judgment as well as promise. In the minds of the optimists the abolition of slavery was the next step to be taken on the way to the realization of the promise of the kingdom of God on earth. In the minds of the

revival leaders it was a step of repentance, a preparation
for the wrath to come. Like an ancient prophet Samuel
Hopkins had warned Congress in 1776 that the wrath of
heaven would fall upon a nation which, claiming for itself
the rights of liberty, refused to grant them to the slaves.[49]
The keynote of Finney's influence upon the antislavery
movement was his preaching of immediate repentance
and immediate restitution. Weld's vision of the wrath to
come was even more vivid than his millennial hope. The
great fire in New York was to his mind the herald sent to
announce the coming of a host, for

the land is full of blood. . . . The poor have cried and ears have
been stopped and hearts have been steeled; and avarice has
clutched the last pittance, and lust has gored itself with spoil,
and prejudice has spurned God's image with loathing, and pas-
sion has rushed upon the helpless and trodden down the needy
in the gates; and when iniquity has been visited by terrible re-
buke, it has swelled with pride and gnashed with rage, and
cursed the poor and blasphemed God — scorning repentance
and defying wrath to the uttermost. . . . What can save us as a
nation but repentance — immediate, profound, *public*, proclaimed abroad, wide as our infamy and damning guilt have
gone!

Such repentance must be not an affair of lamentations
but of confession and restoration to the uttermost, " loos-
ing the bonds, undoing the burdens, breaking every yoke,
dealing bread to the hungry, hiring the poor that are cast
out, and satisfying the afflicted soul. This may save us.
God grant it may not be too late! " [50]

It was too late, even in 1835.   The repentance of America failed, the method of the Christian revolution was rejected, by the north as by the south.   The coming kingdom was hastened by a millennialism which sang the " Battle Hymn of the Republic," and when the new day came it was no reign of peace and brotherhood: it was called Reconstruction.   Instead of the supper of the Lord in the kingdom of heaven America celebrated its " Great Barbecue." [51]

The issue of the Civil War increased the hope of the coming kingdom among men who identified it with the cause of the north.   To others the war proved that the hope of the kingdom on earth was dependent on the progress of Christ's kingdom.   It remained for Samuel Harris in his influential lectures on the *Kingdom of Christ on Earth*, delivered in 1870, to express and systematize the hopes of the Evangelical movement in America for a transformation of the social life.   Rejecting literal millenarianism he also rejected its secularized and humanistic form.   " The kingdom of Christ is not originated and advanced by the spontaneous development of humanity; but a redeeming power comes down upon humanity from God, and enters into human history as an always working energy, quickening men to spiritual life and transforming society into the kingdom of God."   This power is concentrated in no organization.   The kingdom of Christ is not the visible church, but the spirit and life which express themselves imperfectly in visible societies.   Neither is it civilization, for that also is a relative thing.   Yet civilizations can be made Christian by the power of the redemption. The coming kingdom is no spiritual estate removed from contact with political and economic life; it is again life changed at its center and changed therefore also at its circumference, in all its relations. He shares the glowing hope of the triumph of this kingdom, though with due recognition of the fact that its coming is no matter of automatic progress but of divine activity and human work made effective by conversion of the hearts.

If each successive age of the Christian era has had some specific doctrine of Christianity to develop, that which is given to this generation to study and unfold is the Christian doctrine of Christ's kingdom as the reign of righteousness and love over all the earth in the life and civilization of men. . . . And in view of both the thinking and the practical life and character of the age I believe that no preceding age has presented conditions so favorable to the advancement of Christ's kingdom and so encouraging to faithful Christian effort.[52]

When the social gospel appeared toward the end of the century it came as the heir of this living movement which had proceeded in dialectical fashion from individual to communal hope. How evangelical Gladden's conception of the coming kingdom was, how much his hope was based on the success of Christ's coming, appears in his address "Where Is the Kingdom of God?": "This kingdom that we find, here on the earth, steadily widening its borders and strengthening its dominion; growing as the dawn grows toward the perfect day that is not yet; . . .

this kingdom is itself a mighty witness of a Power that makes for righteousness, of a God whose name is Love." One striking truth connected with this kingdom is that the signs of its coming " are visible only in those parts of the world where Jesus Christ is known and loved as Master and Lord." The kingdom of God " can be traced as directly to Jesus Christ as the St. Lawrence river can be traced to its source in the mighty inland sea. . . . The words of Christ are the law of this kingdom; the spirit of Christ is the life of this kingdom." [53] That Rauschenbusch was also largely dependent upon the evangelical tradition is becoming increasingly evident.[54]

Yet the evangelical doctrine of the kingdom was not adequate for the new situation in which these men found themselves. It could not emancipate itself from the conviction — more true in its time than in ours — that the human unit is the individual. It was unable therefore to deal with social crisis, with national disease and the misery of human groups. It continued to think of crisis in terms of death while it had begun to think of promise in social terms. It tended, moreover, to become more and more institutionalized. So reaction against the evangelical doctrine of the kingdom needed to arise among its own children. Nevertheless they remained the heirs of its experience and its promise.

In all their search for the redeeming word which might direct misery on the way to joy, turn injustice toward righteousness and send warring men down the paths of peace Gladden, Rauschenbusch and their colleagues carried with them a vision and a promise which had been written not on stone or paper but on fleshly tables of the heart by a fresh and nation-wide experience of the resurrection. Their fathers believed that Christ was risen from the dead and was in the midst of men not only because they had read the story of the empty tomb; they believed in his coming to rule in righteousness and peace not because they had calculated the meaning of Daniel's cryptic numbers and the Revelation's strange prognostications. They believed because they had seen, though in a glass darkly, and having seen they were ready to count their present security as loss that they might know him and the power of his resurrection in the whole life of men. So their children were directed to march in their own time toward the coming kingdom not by a rationalism which regarded cross and resurrection, redemption and atonement, as ancient superstitions, or by liberalism which denied the divine sovereignty, but by their memory of a loyalty to the kingdom of God which has not been ashamed of the gospel.

V

INSTITUTIONALIZATION AND SECULARIZATION OF THE KINGDOM

THE KINGDOM of God in America is neither an ideal nor an organization. It is a movement which, like the city of God described by Augustine in ancient times, appears in only partial and mixed manner in the ideas and institutions in which men seek to fix it. In that movement we vaguely discern a pattern — one which is not like the plan of a building or any static thing, but more like the pattern of a life, a poem or of other things dynamic. It is a New World symphony in which each movement has its own specific theme, yet builds on all that has gone before and combines with what follows so that the meaning of the whole can be apprehended only as the whole is heard. If one listens only to measures and phrases and bars, no pattern can be apparent.

The first symphonic movement developed the theme of the sovereignty of God in many variations. There were discords and clashing of cymbals and some solo flights by wayward players in the orchestra, yet all were carried by and united in the persistent strains of the first violins. The second movement began with the theme of Christ's kingdom for which the first part had prepared the listeners. Sometimes only a fragment of the theme was sounded; a counter-theme of human kingdoms was developed; the movement was interrupted by rumbling kettledrums suggestive of internal strife. Yet the unity of the composition was maintained as crude instruments, fashioned in the backwoods and played by amateurs, reasserted the theme of the dominion of the Lord. The third movement was allegro. Though it began with forewarnings of doom a strain of hope lifted itself out of the morbid sounds and grew in power and completeness until it dominated the great polyphony of New World life.

Our allegory fails us at many points. The kingdom of God in America is not wholly describable in terms of movement. For there were pauses in the process, moments of petrifaction when the living current was frozen into rigidity. And there was loss of memory; what had gone before was forgotten and men began to move without remembrance of their point of departure or of their plan of march.

I. INSTITUTIONALIZING THE KINGDOM

Professor Henri Bergson has described religion as " the crystallization, brought about by a scientific process of cooling, of what mysticism had poured, while hot, into the soul of man." [1] The statement is subject to many criticisms, since it may be objected that the term " religion " is as applicable to the dynamic process as it is to the crystallized product, that the process of cooling is not always scientific, that prophetism more than mysticism represents the dynamic element in Christianity, and that the molten fluid is poured into the social life rather than into individual souls. Nevertheless the philosopher of vitalism has described a process which had become unintelligible to modern men when it was set forth in the traditional terms of gospel and law, but which is a very real part of all religious life.

The occasional crystallization or institutionalization of the kingdom of God movement is apparently inevitable. The prophets' conviction of the divine sovereignty as a living reality, their experience of judgment and hope of salvation were conserved by legal Judaism in such fashion that the vitality of prophetic faith was denied. The living Christianity of the apostolic period was made concrete in the rituals, organizations, disciplines and creeds of the Greek and Roman churches. The religious renaissance of the twelfth and thirteenth centuries came to a stop in scholastic theology and ecclesiastical institutions. What happened in the earlier eras was repeated in the history of European Protestantism. On the Continent the Reformation came to its conclusion with the establishment of state churches, systems of pure doctrine and conventionalized Christian conduct. The " glorious revolution " in England marked the beginning of the Georgian era in church as well as state. What had occurred elsewhere with monotonous regularity could not be prevented in America. Here also Puritanism and Quakerism, the Awakening and the revivals, poured white-hot convictions into the souls of men, only to have these cool off into crystallized codes, solidified institutions, petrified creeds.

Such phenomena of institutionalization always have an ambiguous character. On the one hand they are genuine efforts to conserve for post-revolutionary generations the gains made by a revolutionary movement. By reducing prophetic ethics to a code Judaism was enabled to teach it to the children who had not seen the Lord with Isaiah nor heard with Amos the thundering approach of the hosts of wrath. By committing that code to the watchful care of a professional group it could enforce the conduct called for by the seers. Henceforth the nation had been made secure against lapsing again into the idolatry and disloyal conduct which had called forth the protests of Hosea and Jeremiah. So also the creeds, rites, offices and discipline of the early Christian churches made it possible for them to lead second generation Christians into the communion with the Father and the Son which their parents had received as a surprising gift, and to the experience of forgiveness and brotherly love which had come as a revolutionary event into the lives of the early disciples. The same thing is true of the later crystallizations of Christian movements. They all consolidated the gains of revolutionary epochs and put them into forms that could be transmitted to children and children's children. Without such stabilization and conservation the great movements would have passed like storms at sea, leaving behind them nothing but the wreckage of the earlier establishments they had destroyed.

Yet institutions can never conserve without betraying the movements from which they proceed. The institution is static whereas its parent movement had been dynamic; it confines men within its limits while the movement had liberated them from the bondage of institutions; it looks to the past, the movement had pointed forward. Though in content the institution resembles the dynamic epoch whence it proceeded, in spirit it is like the state before the revolution. So the Christian church, after the early period, often seemed more closely related in attitude to the Jewish synagogue and the Roman state than to the age of Christ and his apostles; its creed was often more like a system of philosophy than like the living gospel. Post-Reformation Lutheranism and Calvinism resembled, in their efforts to control belief and conduct and in their self-assured bearing, the Catholicism with which they fought. It is ever so, in politics and in learning no less than in religion. The situation is not explicable in terms of a philosophy of progress which maintains that " they must upwards still and onwards who would keep abreast of truth." For the failure of the institution is not simply due to its inability to keep pace with a changing cultural environment; frequently it is more adaptable to its setting than the revolutionary movement had been. It seems rather to lack inner vitality; it is without spontaneity and the power to originate new ideas; it is content with past achievement and more afraid of loss than it is hopeful of new insight or strength; it is on the defensive. Institutions, however, differ not only in spirit from their parent movements; they tend also to change the content which they are trying to conserve. When the great insights of a creative time are put into the symbolic form of words, formulas and creeds, much must always be omitted. The symbol is never the reality and it is subject to progressive loss of meaning; in time it often comes to take the place of the experience to which it had originally pointed. So by limitation and loss of symbolic reference, and by the substitution of the static for the dynamic, institutions deny what they wish to affirm and become the antithesis to their own thesis. The antithesis is never complete; something is always conserved, but much is lost and repudiated.

This universal process from which there seems to be no escape in time is illustrated by the history of the kingdom of God in America at more than one point. Something of the tendency toward petrifaction manifests itself, indeed, throughout the movement; a downward drag accompanies the whole aspiration as those who are ever fearful of disaster attempt to halt the march and to establish safe camping places. At two points, however, the tendency toward institutionalization becomes particularly manifest: first, in the time of second and third generation Puritans and Quakers and second, in the period after the Awakening and the revivals.

The conservative interest showed itself in the earlier period in the adoption of the Half-Way Covenant and of Stoddardeanism by Puritans and of birthright membership by the Society of Friends. Apart from the political considerations which made the first of these measures desirable, all three of them represented genuine efforts to make available for new generations the church fellowship which their fathers had enjoyed and to maintain the influence of faith in the sovereignty of God and in the kingdom of Christ.[2]

Moreover they were necessary for children who, having been bred in the doctrines and discipline of the church, could not be expected to receive the faith with the ardor their parents had manifested nor to experience in a second birth what had in their case been given them in large part with the first. The revolution was past and it was not wise to expect of the post-revolutionary generation the same reconstruction of life which a revolutionary time had required. Still, the effect of these measures was to convert the society of the loyalists of the kingdom into a complacent organization with convictions less and less pronounced and a discipline less and less rigorous. The sovereignty of God was no longer the dynamic activity of the being who created, judged and saved mankind in every moment of time; it was now rather the rule of his laws, while the kingdom of Christ came to mean either the present church on earth or heaven with its eternal rewards.

The typical representative of post-revolutionary Puritanism was Cotton Mather, who is so often and so unfortunately used as an example of Puritanism itself. Good conservative that he was, much of the old loyalty to the divine sovereignty is manifest in him; yet in what perverted form! Parrington has written that " in the egocentric universe wherein Cotton Mather lived and labored the cosmos had shrunk to the narrow bounds of a Puritan commonwealth whereof Boston was the capital and the prosperity of the North Church the special and particular object of divine concern." [3] The statement may be paraphrased with respect to the kingdom of God, for this had been reduced for Cotton Mather to the dominion of the English Reformation, and of that Reformation Boston was the chief glory. " Boston," he exclaimed, " thou hast been lifted up to heaven! " [4] He looked to the past, to the incomparable institutions of the fathers, to the Sabbath day ordinances, the Congregational order and discipline, and the laws of the commonwealth. With all his eagerly displayed learning he defended the established order which, in his estimation, came nearer to perfection than any other Christian society in the world. Not only had the kingdom of God become an institution but the reign of Christ had become a habit. The law written upon the inward parts was for Cotton Mather an inscription to be endlessly studied in a state of hypochondriac introspection. His *Essays To Do Good* [5] are a classic example of inverted moralism. Here all attention is directed toward the self and its moral culture. The brave objectivism of the early Puritans which demanded only that God's will be done is turned into febrile subjectivism which evermore asks whether the heart of the doer is good. The message of the kingdom of Christ is translated into a new, spiritualized version of the law, as exacting in its demands, as minutely defined and hedged about and as full of temptations to Pharisaism as any external legal code ever was. Against the codified, formalized and institutionalized conceptions of the sovereignty of God and the kingdom of Christ secular liberalism was bound to rebel. The Yankee spirit with its objective common sense offered a happy alternative to this ingrown Puritanism.[6] Yet it was Edwards rather than Franklin and the Great Awakening rather than the rational enlightenment which really broke the fetters of petrified Puritanism and restored dynamic to the Christian church.

The fate which overtook the earlier movement could not be evaded, however, by its successor. The Awakening also lapsed into slumber as the attempt was made to conserve the gains which it had brought. At the beginning of the nineteenth century the standing order in Connecticut, represented especially by Timothy Dwight and Lyman Beecher, reproduced the spirit of Cotton Mather, though the content of their creed was Edwardean. As the century went on the process of crystallization continued; the creeping paralysis extended from Connecticut to the frontiers, until all of the orders of American " friars " had become denominations and all the denominations began to defend their glorious past, their creeds and conventions. Compared with the movement out of which it proceeded this institutional faith was characterized above all by the absence of the sense of crisis which had always been present in the movement. Stated positively, the conventional faith was marked by the conviction that the crisis was past and that the main concern of men should be the conservation of its fruits.

Edwards, Hopkins, Whitefield, Finney knew the sovereignty of God as the present activity and initiative of the being on whom every man in every moment was infinitely dependent. The sovereign God of Lyman Beecher and his colleagues is an absentee monarch who declared his will in a remote past and caused it to be recorded in irrefrangible laws. To live under the sovereignty, as these church leaders seem to conceive it, is to live not in relation to divine being but in obedience to law. They would interpret the fall of an apple from the tree not as due to the attraction of the large mass for the small but as an act in obedience to the law of gravity. At all events in religion they define the decrees of God as " his determination to create a universe of free agents, to exist forever under the perfect laws of his moral government, perfectly administered; for the gratification and manifestation of his benevolence, for the perfect enjoyment of all his obedient subjects: with all that is implied therein and all the consequences foreseen." [7] The sense of critical immediate relations between man and the Being of beings has been lost in the feeling that man is responsible for keeping certain laws. Moreover these laws are conceived to have been once and for all established in nature and published in the Bible, so that the latter comes to be a book of statutes rather than an aid to the understanding of God's living will.[8] It is not only the Bible which mediates the moral government of God, for the religious institutions founded upon that statute book may claim to represent his sovereignty also. Lyman Beecher tends to identify the moral law of God with the law of New England Puritanism and the latter with the law of the United States.

> Our own republic [he declares] in its Constitution and laws is of heavenly origin. It was not borrowed from Greece or Rome, but from the Bible. Where we borrowed a ray from Greece or Rome, stars and suns were borrowed from another source — the Bible. There is no position more susceptible of proof than that, as the moon borrows from the sun her light, so our Constitution borrows from the Bible, its elements, proportions and power. It was God that gave these elementary principles to our fore-fathers, as the " pillar of fire by night, and the cloud by day," for their guidance. All the liberty the world ever knew is but a dim star to the noon-day sun which is poured on man by these oracles of heaven.[9]

Beecher reserves his most glowing praise for the laws of New England. " Behold," he exclaims, " their institutions, such as the world needs and attended as they have been by the power of God, able to enlighten and renovate the world." [10]   The church organization of New England is " the noblest edifice ever reared by divine and human cooperation ";[11] " the Sabbath is the great organ of the divine administration — the only means provided by God to give ubiquity and power to his moral government." [12] So Beecher rallies men to " the standard which our fathers reared " and " to institutions of heaven, provided to aid us in fleeing from the wrath to come." [13]

When the sovereignty of God has been reduced to a

code of laws established in the past all the ideas connected with it at a time when it was experienced as living reality become unintelligible. To an Edwards, aware of infinite dependence on the Being of beings, God's absolute agency in all things is a glorious and self-evident truth, while it is equally self-evident that man must and does struggle to respond to the divine initiative. When God's sovereignty has become a law and the living relation a mechanical one, the dialogue between God and man is dissolved into a statement of incompatible doctrines. Man, it is said, is completely determined; man, it is claimed, is free to obey or disobey. The dialectic becomes a debate in which men shout their dogmas at one another and sometimes make slight concessions, such as that God does not wholly determine man or that man is not quite free; and such concessions are called " improvements in divinity." What could be truly said of a living process becomes untrue or unintelligible when it is asserted of the petrified product. Institutionalized faith, seeking to conserve the insights of prophetic experience, reduces the sovereign God to a law and his activity to that of fate. So the divine determinism of an Edwards becomes fatalism in his successors.

In similar fashion the post-revival period confined the kingdom of Christ within the walls of the visible church. "The church as a collective body," says Beecher, " is the organ of God's moral administration — a chartered community, formed for the special purpose of giving efficacy and perpetuity to the revealed laws of the divine government "; it is the executive arm of God's moral government, even as the Bible is the legislative organ. It is " the divine practical system for accomplishing the salvation of the world "; it is an association for " mutual defense and increased efficiency in the propagation of religion." [14]   Here we have that very definition of the church of which dynamic Protestantism had been afraid; the church has become a self-conscious representative of God which instead of pointing men to him points them first of all to itself.   Naturally it turns to the defensive under the circumstances; now it must justify and praise itself, its gospel and its faith, instead of living in the forgiveness of sin, doing its work and making its confession.

In the area of practice the institutionalization of the kingdom of Christ became even more fateful.   The evangelization movement had attempted to conserve and develop the results of conversion by organizing converts into societies, by requiring these to exercise supervision over their members and by encouraging them to undertake further evangelization.   Such societies reflected the peculiar interests, prejudices and convictions of leaders or of social groups, and were as different from one another as Franciscans were from Dominicans or as both were from Jesuits.   Under the influence of the Awakening and the revivals divisions also took place in the established churches.   Yet there was a great deal of hearty cooperation and it was definitely understood that the organization of churches or societies was quite secondary to the common work of extending the kingdom of Christ.

Moreover the various groups and leaders were conscious of participating in a single great movement, though their work lay in different areas among people of varying traditions and was advanced by different methods. The social divergences between the churches or societies were not sufficient to conquer this sense of community.[15] Speaking of the first Awakening Leonard W. Bacon remarks that in " the glow of the revival the Continent awoke to the consciousness of a common religious life " and, since the movement was international in origin as well as in effect, American Christians became highly aware under its influence of the ecumenical character of the faith. The effect of the second revival was similar; American religious life, though divided among many groups, took on a common pattern, exhibited a common interest and was inspired by a common hope.

With the cessation of the movement and the turn to institutionalism the aggressive societies became denominations, for that peculiar institution, the American denomination, may be described as a missionary order which has turned to the defensive and lost its consciousness of the invisible catholic church. These orders now confused themselves with their cause and began to promote themselves, identifying the kingdom of Christ with the practices and doctrines prevalent in the group. Though the content of the institutionalized faith seemed to be like that of the movement, its spirit was utterly different. As Congregationalists and Presbyterians became self-conscious and more aware of their differing heritages

than of their common task they dropped their plan of
union and entered into competition with each other.
The missionary enterprise, home and foreign, was divided along denominational lines; every religious society
became intent upon promoting its own peculiar type of
work in religious education, in the evangelization of
youth, in theological education, in the printing and distribution of religious literature. Cordial relations, such
as had existed between Lutherans and Reformed, between the latter and the Congregationalist and Presbyterian churches, and among revival groups on the frontier
gave way to keen competition. With the loss of the
sense of the common task in proclaiming the kingdom of
Christ, sectional, racial and cultural differences assumed
increasing importance. The more attention was concentrated upon the church the greater became the tendency toward schism. It is difficult to assign a date to
this development of institutionalism. In New England
Congregationalism it reappeared during the Jeffersonian
period; in general it manifested itself particularly in the
fourth decade of the century and from then on became
increasingly important as the impetus of the original
movement was progressively lost.[16]

The institutionalization of the kingdom of Christ was
naturally accompanied by its nationalization. For with
attention directed to the self with its peculiar advantages,
heritage and mission, with the turn from aggression and
confession to defense and apologetic and with the increasing confusion of church and world, it was natural

that contact with ecumenical Christianity should be lost. The old idea of American Christians as a chosen people who had been called to a special task was turned into the notion of a chosen nation especially favored. In Lyman Beecher, as in Cotton Mather before him, we have seen how this tendency came to expression. As the nineteenth century went on the note of divine favoritism was increasingly sounded. Christianity, democracy, Americanism, the English language and culture, the growth of industry and science, American institutions — these are all confounded and confused. The contemplation of their own righteousness filled Americans with such lofty and enthusiastic sentiments that they readily identified it with the righteousness of God. The crisis of the kingdom of the Christ was passed; it occurred in the democratic revolution, or in the birth of modern science, or in the evangelical revival, or in the Protestant Reformation. Henceforth the kingdom of the Lord was a human possession, not a permanent revolution.[17] It is in particular the kingdom of the Anglo-Saxon race, which is destined to bring light to the gentiles by means of lamps manufactured in America. Thus institutionalism and imperialism, ecclesiastical and political, go hand in hand.

As the kingdom of Christ is institutionalized in church and state the ways of entering it are also defined, mapped, motorized and equipped with guard rails.[18] Regeneration, the dying to the self and the rising to new life — now apparently sudden, now so slow and painful, so confused, so real, so mixed — becomes conversion which takes place on Sunday morning during the singing of the last hymn or twice a year when the revival preacher comes to town. There is still reality in it for some converts but, following a prescribed pattern for the most part in its inception and progress, the life has gone out of it. It is not so much the road from the temporal to the eternal, from trust in the finite to faith in the infinite, from self-centeredness to God-centeredness, as it is the way into the institutional church or the company of respectable Christian churchmen who keep the Sabbath, pay their debts promptly, hope for heaven and are never found drunk either with sensual or with spiritual excitement. What happened to conversion is strikingly indicated by a somewhat curious book written in the eighteen-thirties for the instruction of English Christians by an American clergyman, Calvin Colton. He distinguishes between two sorts of revivals, " one when the instruments are not apparent; the other when the instruments are obvious." The former simply come; one waits for them as for rain, and this, he says, " till a few years past, was the more ordinary character of revivals of religion in America. . . . It is only within a few years, that the promotion of revivals by human instruments, has to a considerable extent been made a subject of study, and an object of systematic effort." Now revivals " are made matters of human calculation, by the arithmetic of faith in God's engagement." God may work when his people sleep but he never sleeps when his people work.[19] The Great Awakening had become a method for rousing God from slumber.

The method which Colton naïvely set forth, and which indeed Finney had tended to prepare, continued to develop until it reached its climax in " Billy " Sunday's manipulation of mass suggestion. In a new form the institutionalism and sacramentalism against which Protestantism had originally rebelled asserted themselves. Church and religion were confused with the center and fountain of being, and their means of grace became the sole instruments through which God was allowed to work. Moreover the new ecclesiasticism was less beautiful and often less wise than the old had been.

Moralistic ideas were closely associated with this mechanical conception of conversion. To be reconciled to God now meant to be reconciled to the established customs of a more or less Christianized society. As the Christian church became the protector of the social mores so its revivals tended to become instruments for enforcing the prevailing standards. As it became increasingly clear how perilous the use of liquor was in democratic and industrial society the revival was used especially to combat this evil. Men were now saved not from the frustration, conflict, futility and poverty of life which they sought to escape in the saloons; they were saved from whisky. And the revivals were sometimes used in less evidently useful ways, to enforce the codes of capitalist industry, to overcome the rebellion of workers and to foster the bourgeois virtues on which the success of the industrial system depended.

Petrifaction also assailed the life of hope. As the

sovereignty of God was institutionalized in laws, the kingdom of Christ in denominations and means of grace, so the strain toward the coming kingdom and the hope of its coming were transformed into a moral sanction or into a belief in progress. As a hope of the individual the coming kingdom became an otherworldly event not organically related to the present. Hell became a prison to which a divine judge committed the citizens who had failed to observe the laws, and heaven a reward for good deeds done. Punishment and reward were as externally related to life as monetary wages are to labor and fines to misdemeanors. The doctrine of crisis became an instrument for enforcing the mores of a Christian, democratic, bourgeois society. As is the habit of unskillful parents and legislators, the preachers of this defensive faith increased their threats and made their promises the more alluring the worse the behavior of the children became; and the greater the threats and promises the more doubtful of their fulfillment were the children. If the crisis was thought of in terms of the end of all mundane things it was again dealt with in the mechanical and literalist fashion of those who had forgotten the reality while retaining the symbol. Doubtless there was a good deal of genuine awareness of the critical character of human life in the Millerite movement and in later millenarian fundamentalism, but on the whole they seem to have been more interested in symbols than in meanings and their preparation for the coming kingdom was usually as irrelevant to the actual issues of life as was the crisis itself.

Insofar as the kingdom was conceived in social terms the faith in its coming was transformed into a belief in progress. The judgment was really past. It had occurred in a democratic revolution. The life now lived in the land of promise was regarded as the promised life, and no greater bliss seemed possible for men than was afforded by the extension of American institutions to all the world. That America itself would need to meet the ever coming kingdom as a judgment upon itself, or that the American church would ever need to pass through new catastrophes and resurrections, was not even remotely suggested. The self-congratulatory tone appeared even in the youthful Bushnell, who took it for " granted that complete Protestantism is pure Christianity," while Protestantism in its complete form is congregationalism and congregationalism is the author of republicanism. "We are the depositaries of that light," he cried, "which is to illuminate the world." [20] Whether conceived in political or ecclesiastical or economic or cultural terms, the coming kingdom is never regarded as involving both death and resurrection, both crisis and promise, but only as the completion of tendencies now established.

When the social gospel appeared at the end of the nineteenth century this institutionalized view of the coming kingdom was one of its ingredients. Since the social gospel movement was a multifarious thing, it may be truer to say that one of the parties which called for the application of Christianity to the social life had in mind above all the conservation and extension of American political and ecclesiastical institutions. Many of the reformers seem to have been interested at this point. In the days of the slavery conflict they had indicated little interest in slaves, but a profound concern for the conservation of institutions threatened by the political power of the slaveholder and a great desire to extend their own patterns of life over the whole country. Now they often seemed less interested in the worker than in winning him to the church, that is, of using the social gospel as a means for the maintenance of the institution. As reformers they turned, when persuasion failed, to political means, in order that good social habits of temperance and Sabbath observance might be maintained. As propagandists they sought the extension of democratic institutions — if necessary by recourse to military force — in order that all the world might share in the blessings of the kingdom of God on earth.

In these and other ways the faith in the kingdom was institutionalized. Having achieved some construction it became content with its achievements and displayed a self-confidence and a self-righteousness which could not but call forth reaction on the part of those who discerned how relative and confining were the institutions which claimed universal validity as well as heavenly origin.

II. LIBERALISM AND THE KINGDOM OF GOD

When liberalism arose in American religion it found its foe not in dynamic Christianity but rather in these orthodox institutions and established beliefs which were the crystallized products of the Protestant movement. Liberalism represented again a dynamic element in religious life; it was a revolt against the fatalism into which the faith in divine sovereignty had been congealed, against the biblicism which made the Scriptures a book of laws for science and for morals, against the revivalism which reduced regeneration to a method for drumming up church members, and against the otherworldliness which had made heaven and hell a reward and a punishment.

In dealing with liberalism we need, however, to be as much on our guard as in speaking of Calvinism. Not everything that assumed the name was dynamic. There was as great a difference between the liberalisms of Andrews Norton and of William Ellery Channing as there was between the Calvinisms of Cotton Mather and of Jonathan Edwards. Rationalistic liberalism as represented by the Deists in England, the rationalists of France and their few American followers, was as static in its conceptions and as self-righteous in its attitudes as the ecclesiastical orthodoxy it opposed. The Nature which it tended to substitute for the orthodox God was also a fixed and mechanical reality; its laws, like the decrees of the institutionalized deity, were not approximate statements about a free and living activity but the statutes by which a constitutional monarch was confined and bound. Its truths of reason, like the orthodox truths of revelations, were regarded not as abstract utterances about concrete reality but as precise ideas to which being was re-

quired to conform.   It was interested in the doctrine of
human freedom as religious institutionalism was interested in the doctrine of predestination, but it was as little
concerned with the winning of liberty as the latter was
with the realization of man's infinite dependence.   Soci-
ologically this so-called liberalism was connected with the
defense of the interests of the property-holding, rising
middle classes, as orthodoxy was connected with the interests of the socially established clergy and the new
liberalism with the aspirations of the great mass of little
men.   When it appeared in America in religious form it
was found among the wealthy and refined, not among the
followers of Jefferson.   They did not desire the extension
of freedom but resented the interference of orthodoxy in
their affairs, its evident crudities of thought and its threat
to their religious security.

The dynamic liberalism of which Channing and
Emerson were the great American protagonists was more
akin in spirit to the Evangelical movement than to this
earlier rationalistic liberalism.   It shared with the religious enlightenment, if indeed it did not partly derive
from it, the sense of man's vital relationship to the reality
which overarched him, out of which he came and to
which he returned.   It called that reality Nature or Over-
soul, whereas faith, relying upon revelation, conceived it
in personal terms and looked askance at this pantheism.
But the relation to the real was in both cases immediate
and urgent.   Moreover, Transcendentalism, like the
Evangelical movement, saw all the world as sacred be-

cause of its relation to the ultimate being. Channing confesses: " All my sentiments and affections have lately changed. I once considered mere moral attainment as the only object I had to pursue. I have now solemnly given myself up to God. I consider supreme love to him as the first of all duties, and morality seems but a branch from the vigorous root of religion. I love mankind because they are the children of God." [21] The statement must not be overemphasized since Channing tends on the whole to emphasize human dignity and worth for their own sakes, yet the connection was there. In Emerson it is even more apparent, for the haunting sense of the One which expresses itself in the Many, of the universal mind of which each individual is an incarnation, lies back of almost every sentence that he writes. In this sacred world Transcendentalism like Evangelicalism again turns eagerly to works of philanthropy. Channing summarizes the faith which lies back of his endeavors for social reform in words which an Evangelical might have uttered:

I have also felt and continually insisted that a new reverence for man was essential to the cause of social reform. As long as men regard one another as they do now, that is as little better than brutes, they will continue to treat one another brutally. Each will strive by craft or skill to make others his tools. There can be no spirit of brotherhood, no true peace, any farther than men come to understand their affinity with and relation to God and the infinite purpose for which he gave them life. As yet these ideas are treated as a kind of spiritual romance; and the teacher who really expects men to see in themselves and one

another the children of God is smiled at as a visionary. The re-
ception of this plainest truth of Christianity would revolutionize
society and create relations among men not dreamed of at the
present day.[22]

Evangelicals had expressed the idea in a different way:
they had spoken of their brothers as those for whom God
had sent his Son into the world, that through great suffering he might show and exercise his love for them; they
had spoken of the need for that redemptive work. They
had never intended to say, as liberalism looking at orthodoxy thought, that because God loved man despite man's
wickedness men were entitled to demean mankind.

In other ways also dynamic liberalism was akin to
dynamic Evangelicalism. It saw an intimate connection
between man's behavior and its results. In the idea of
compensation it contradicted the thought of externally
related rewards and punishments to which institutionalized faith had reduced the original Christian awareness
that man, living under the sovereignty of God, must reap
what he sows. It desired also a certain regeneration of
the central principle in man rather than a reform of overt
behavior or an attachment to different institutions.
What man most wishes, says Emerson,

is to be lifted to some higher platform, that he may see beyond
his present fear the transalpine good, so that his fear, his cold-
ness, his custom, may be broken up like fragments of ice, melted
and carried away in the great stream of good will. . . . The
criticism and attack on institutions, which we have witnessed, has
made one thing plain, that society gains nothing whilst a man,

not himself renovated, attempts to renovate things around him: he has become tediously good in some particular, but negligent or narrow in the rest: and hypocrisy and vanity are often the disgusting result.[28]

In spirit and even in language this sounds like an Evangelical attack upon the merely moral man.

What made the two movements most akin, however, was their common interest in liberty. For Transcendentalism and Romanticism liberty was not so much a right or series of rights as spontaneity; hence its love of genius and its cult of originality. Liberty was a good to be won rather than a possession to be prized; its extension to all men through the elimination of chattel slavery, the increase of education, the restraint of governmental and of economic masters and the provision of economic security became its increasing concern. These interests brought it into continuous conflict with the defenders of established institutions, whether these were the products of rationalist liberalism or of Calvinism and Evangelicalism. The conflict was not between ideas but rather between dead tradition, no matter what its content, and the living tradition.

The similarities between the two movements extended to their attitudes toward the future. It is the fashion nowadays to speak of liberalism as naïvely optimistic. Doubtless it was so. Its naïve optimism appeared in its expectation both of individual and, later, of social salvation. Yet it is often forgotten when the charge is made that this optimism was rooted in the Christian gospel.

The ultimate source of the belief in progress, prevalent for so long a time in the Western world, was not the Darwinian theory of evolution nor the success of science and technology nor yet the expansion of European civilization, though all these reinforced it. The doctrine cannot be traced to the Greeks and to the Renaissance, for the Greeks could think of history only in terms of the recurrent cycles of rebirth and decay imaged in the seasons. Its source was the faith first confessed by the prophets, reaffirmed then in the midst of despair by the apocalypticists, and grounded on a living experience by the apostles of the New Testament. The idea of progress, like the later Marxian view of dialectic materialism, was a secularized version of this theology of history.[24] The liberalism which adopted the idea of progress was historically related to the Evangelicalism which reaffirmed the Hebrew and Christian view of history. Its secularized millenarianism came to expression in the utopian enterprises which founded Brook farms, Oneida communities, New Harmonies and Christian Commonwealth societies, as the more evangelical strain toward the coming kingdom had expressed itself in part in the organization of Philadelphias, Ephratas, Zoars and Amanas.[25] Its vision of the future, as set forth by Edward Bellamy, differed from that which Joseph Bellamy had learned from Edwards and Hopkins as a grandchild may differ from the grandsire. Though liberalism often sought to deny its kinship to the historic gospel its speech and its features betrayed it.

Yet, as the last example indicates, there was conflict as well as affinity between romantic liberalism and Evangelicalism. Though both were dynamic, one was evolutionary, the other revolutionary. The romantic conception of the kingdom of God involved no discontinuities, no crises, no tragedies or sacrifices, no loss of all things, no cross and resurrection. In ethics it reconciled the interests of the individual with those of society by means of faith in a natural identity of interests or in the benevolent, altruistic character of man. In politics and economics it slurred over national and class divisions, seeing only growth of unity and ignoring the increase of self-assertion and exploitation. In religion it reconciled God and man by deifying the latter and humanizing the former. It heard nothing but echoes of childish superstition in the cry for a friendly God and in agonizing confessions of guilt. The conviction that the author and end of all being is a God of love had come to Protestants and Evangelicals, as to Catholic Christians before them, only at great cost as they looked upon the animosity or indifference of that real world which sends each individual back to the dust whence he came, reduces his work to vanity and buries the tragic empires beneath rubble and shifting sands. Liberalism, having inherited faith in divine love and human resurrection, held it cheaply; it believed that it could possess by intuition or definition what had been gained only through sacrifice, forgetting that most intuitions are the ideas which men learn before they are five years old and definitions logical devices to which reality is not bound to conform. It no longer knew that religion, as Professor Whitehead has described it in a great phrase, is " transition from God the void to God the enemy and from God the enemy to God the companion." [26] It began and ended with the companion. Neither man with his bigger and better wars, his slums and mining villages, his massive iniquity, nor God with his wrath interposed any barriers to the constant intercourse of the finite and the infinite, the sinful and the holy. For an Edwards divine sovereignty had been a hard truth to which he had slowly learned to adjust his thought and life; for liberalism it was an untruth. It established continuity between God and man by adjusting God to man.

Since no reconciliation to the divine sovereign was necessary the reign of Christ, in the new interpretation, involved no revolutionary events in history or the life of individuals. Christ the Redeemer became Jesus the teacher or the spiritual genius in whom the religious capacities of mankind were fully developed. Moreover the radical revolution at the center of life for which dynamic Protestantism and Evangelicalism had contended seemed unnecessary to a liberalism which objected not only to the identification of this revolution with mechanical conversion but also to the belief that life had been corrupted. The renovation of which it spoke was not so much the restoration of health to a diseased body as the clearing out of the accumulated rubbish of traditional beliefs or customs. Evolution, growth, development, the culture of the religious life, the nurture of the kindly sentiments, the extension of humanitarian ideals and the progress of civilization took the place of the Christian revolution.

In similar manner the idea of the coming kingdom was robbed of its dialectical element. It was all fulfillment of promise without judgment. It was thought to be growing out of the present so that no great crisis needed to intervene between the order of grace and the order of glory. In its one-sided view of progress which saw the growth of the wheat but not that of the tares, the gathering of the grain but not the burning of the chaff, this liberalism was indeed naïvely optimistic.

A God without wrath brought men without sin into a kingdom without judgment through the ministrations of a Christ without a cross.

The temper of evolutionary optimism did not prevail in all parts of the liberal movement. There were mediators who shared the protest against static versions of divine sovereignty, salvation and Christian hope but sought nevertheless to retain the critical and dialectical elements in Protestantism. Of these Horace Bushnell was the greatest. His theory of religious education represented protest against the mechanization and formalization of conversion. It also set forth his confidence in the principle of growth. Yet Bushnell recognized the necessity of regeneration.[27] His rejection of Unitarianism and his constant wrestling with the problem of atonement indicate how real for him were the discontinuities in life and how necessary the revolutionary elements in Christianity.²⁸ Though the prevailing tone of his theology was romantic and liberal the Protestant and evangelical note was not lost.

Washington Gladden and Walter Rauschenbusch represented the same mediating tendency in the social gospel movement, and the latter did so more than the former. They distinguished themselves from their liberal contemporaries by keeping relatively close to evangelical notions of the sovereignty of God, of the reign of Christ and of the coming kingdom. In Rauschenbusch especially the revolutionary element remained pronounced; the reign of Christ required conversion and the coming kingdom was crisis, judgment as well as promise. Though his theory of the relation of God and man often seemed liberal he continued to speak the language of the prophets and St. Paul.²⁹

No mediating theology in history has ever been able to keep in balance the opposing elements it seeks to reconcile, and this truth held for the American mediators also. As time went on liberalism began to outweigh Evangelicalism more and more. At the same time the former tended to become increasingly secular or, to speak more accurately, to lose the sense of the broken relation between God and man, between the present and the coming kingdom. In the course of succeeding generations the heritage of faith with which liberalism had started was used up. The liberal children of liberal fathers needed to operate with ever diminishing capital. Channing had revolted against Hopkins, but back of the things Channing said were convictions which Hopkins had held and young Channing had received. In the minds of Channing's hearers also there were rich deposits of evangelical tradition. The faith was operative even where it was not consciously held. Emerson and his hearers, however, had less of the heritage than Channing, Theodore Parker less probably than Emerson. It was so with the succession of mediators. Bushnell protested against the faith he had learned, but he had learned it nevertheless and his protest was significant in part because it arose out of an inner tension between the old and the new. Washington Gladden began where Bushnell left off with less of the consciousness of sovereignty, salvation and redemption than his master had possessed. So the process went on.

The liberal and mediating movement as a whole reflected this loss of the religious heritage. Whatever sense of divine sovereignty the earlier generations had retained, their successors defined God as the object of religion and made this function of the human spiritual life the only executive arm of God's government. It was not God who ruled, but religion ruled a little, and religion needed God for its support. Whatever memory of the gospel of rebirth had been conserved by early romanticism, the later liberalism increasingly identified human values with the divine, proclaimed the glad tidings of progress and hallowed man's moral efforts though they led to civil, international and class war. As youth traveled daily

" farther from the east " the splendid vision of the transalpine good, of the kingdom beyond, faded into the
light of a common day.   The coming kingdom of late
liberalism, like the heaven of senile orthodoxy, came to
be a place not of liberty and glory but of material de-
lights, the modern counterparts of those pleasures which
it had laughed to scorn when it spoke of ancient superstitions.   For the golden harps of the saints it substituted
radios, for angelic wings concrete highways and high-
powered cars, and heavenly rest was now called leisure.
But it was all the same old pattern; only the symbols had
changed.

The same old pattern was repeated also in liberalism's
turn to institutionalism.   It became as intent upon conservation and defense as ever orthodoxy had been.   Its
belief in God, freedom and immortality was no longer a
confession with which to challenge the lesser faiths of
mankind but a precarious doctrine to be anxiously defended by every means which learning and practice put
at one's disposal.   Its means of grace — prayer, worship
and religious education — required the same sort of
apologetic which orthodoxy had used for the defense of
the Scriptures and the Sabbath.   Religion itself needed
to be carefully guarded as a delicate possession which
men might lose, or as a tender plant which required protection against the blighting frost of a scientific world.
Its defenders were thankful for every sop which men of
science threw their way and for every kind word which
the mighty, in universities and halls of government, ven-

tured on its behalf. They sought to prove its usefulness in promoting the dominant purposes of the age or group in which they lived, the purposes of nationalism where nationalism was in power, of capitalism where capitalism reigned, of radicalism where radicalism took the initiative. Defensiveness, of course, was not the only characteristic of institutionalized liberalism. Like static Evangelicalism and static Protestantism it conserved some of the constructive results of past movements. With greater or less success it performed the function which every institutional religion must perform in society, transmitting the best of the mores, qualifying the tendency of life to drop into a practical polytheism, providing hope and improving the morale of men in their hard struggle with themselves and others. Such conservatism led it not infrequently to the adoption of new measures, since an enlightened conservatism knows that the retention of the old is possible only if new forms are used to express the old content. Innovation and improvement, however, are no substitute for constructive and dynamic movement. In institutional liberalism as in institutional Evangelicalism and Protestantism the aggressive movement of the kingdom of God in America had apparently come to a stop. The resources of the faith had been used up or forgotten. An ideal of the coming kingdom, divorced from reliance on the divine initiative and separated from the experience of the Christian revolution, showed itself insufficient to rouse to new life the party of the kingdom of God.

The same institutionalism which represents the death of an old movement can be, as history amply illustrates, the pregnant source of a new aggression. It cannot be otherwise with a church which conserves in some form the gospel of the kingdom of God. At the very time when the paralysis of institutionalization seemed most evident in the Christian movement in America signs were not lacking of a new spirit stirring among the old forms. The restlessness which was abroad, the unchanneled aspirations of youth, the rebellion among the clergy against the institutionalism they had to serve, the active concern for an aggressive Christianity manifested among missionaries and exponents of the social gospel, the deep interest of the Christian Student Movement in a recovery of faith, were indications of a spiritual unrest which might become the seed plot of new life. And it was significant that such movements manifested increasing interest in the great doctrines and traditions of the Christian past, as though they were aware that power had been lost because the heritage had been forgotten, or that there was no way toward the coming kingdom save the way taken by a sovereign God through the reign of Jesus Christ.

NOTES

Introduction

1. Henri Bergson, *The Two Sources of Morality and Religion* (New York, 1935), chap. 2. Cf. E. Durkheim, *The Elementary Forms of Religious Life* (London, 1915), pp. 419 f.; Lucien Lévy-Bruhl, *The "Soul" of the Primitive* (London, 1928).

2. Vernon Louis Parrington, *Main Currents in American Thought* (New York, Harcourt, Brace, 1927-30). Parrington believes we can clear the "fog of biblical disputations" and the "crabbed theology" of Puritans only if "we will resolutely translate the old phrases into modern equivalents, if we will put aside the theology and fasten attention on the politics and the economics of the struggle" (I, 6). The significance of Calvinism becomes clear to anyone "who will take the trouble to translate dogma into political terms" (*ibid.*, p. 13). Roger Williams was "primarily a political philosopher rather than a theologian; religious toleration was only a necessary deduction from the major principles of his political theory" (*ibid.*, p. 66). Jonathan Edwards, interpreted by reference to the social tendencies, was a great anachronism who "followed a path that led back to the absolutist past, rather than forward to a more liberal future" (*ibid.*, pp. 148 f., 156). To social interpreters like Parrington political and economic interests are alone real and the language of politics and economics is the only universal tongue.

3. *Op. cit.*, I, 19.

Chapter I

1. For the Roman Catholic contribution to American life see J. D. G. Shea, *A History of the Catholic Church Within the Limits of the United States* (New York, 1880-92); Thomas O'Gorman, *A History of the Roman Catholic Church in the United States* (New York, 1895); and many excellent studies published by the Catholic University of America. In *The Religious Background of American Culture* (Boston, 1930) T. C. Hall argues that an "old, radical and hardy English Protestantism"

rather than Puritanism, which represented the thought of the Continental Reformation, was the main source of American religion. Since documentary evidence is not available the argument must be supported by many suppositions. Moreover it seems unnecessary to seek historical sources for trends and ideas which arise again and again in Christian history out of similar social situations and human experiences. Insofar as Hall contends for the importance of the sectarian strain in the development of American Christianity the present interpretation largely agrees with him, but it regards that strain as a legitimate expression of the Protestantism of the sixteenth and seventeenth centuries. If the old radical Protestantism of Wyclif survived and came to America it did not escape the profound influence of Puritanism. Even the Quakers are unintelligible save as children of Puritanism.

2. André Siegfried, *America Comes of Age* (New York, 1927), p. 33.

3. *Contra Gentiles*, III, 37; *Compendium Theologiae*, chap. 4. Cf. *Summa Theologica*, Part II, QQ. I–V.

4. K. E. Kirk, *The Vision of God. The Christian Doctrine of the Summum Bonum* (London, 1931).

5. Étienne Gilson, *Moral Values and the Moral Life. The System of Thomas Aquinas*, translated by Leo R. Ward (St. Louis, 1931), pp. 6, 9. Cf. Kirk, *op. cit.*, p. 379; Henri Brémond, *A Literary History of Religious Thought in France* (New York, 1928–) I, 10 f.

6. *Summa Theologica*, Part I, Q. CIII, art. 6. Cf. Q. CIV, art. 2, where St. Thomas writes: " A thing is kept in being by that which gives it being. But God gives being by certain intermediate causes. Therefore he also keeps things in being by means of certain causes. . . . God created all things immediately, but in the creation itself he established an order among things, so that some depend on others by which they are preserved in being, though he remains the principal cause of their preservation."

7. Calvin, *Institutes of the Christian Religion*, Book I, chap. 5, paragraph v. Cf. Walther von Loewenich, *Luthers Theologia Crucis* (München, 1929), pp. 88 ff.

8. *Institutes*, Book III, chap. 7, paragraph i.

9. Ernst Benz, *Ecclesia Spiritualis. Kirchenidee und Geschichtstheologie der Franziskanischen Reformation* (Stuttgart, 1934), p. 164.

10. Adolph Harnack, *History of Dogma* (London, 1894–99), I, 162 ff., especially n. 1, pp. 167 ff.; and *Monasticism: Its Ideals and History* (London, 1901).

11. The Augsburg Confession defined Christian perfection as follows: " Christian perfection is this, to fear God sincerely, and again, to con-

ceive great faith, and to trust assuredly that God is pacified toward us, for Christ's sake; to ask and certainly to look for help from God in all our affairs, according to our calling; and outwardly to do good works diligently, and to attend to our vocation. In these things doth true perfection and the true worship of God consist: it doth not consist in singleness of life, in beggary, or in vile apparel" (Part I, art. 6). In *Von weltlicher Obrigkeit* Luther wrote, "For perfection and imperfection does not lie in works, nor does it constitute a special outward class among Christians, but it lies in the heart, in faith and love, so that whoever believes and loves more, he is perfect." Ritschl deals with the problem of perfection as defined by Lutheranism in his *Geschichte des Pietismus*, I, 39 ff. Cf. further R. Newton Flew, *The Idea of Perfection in Christian Theology* (London, 1934), chap. 13.

12. Luther, *Von weltlicher Obrigkeit, wie weit man ihr Gehorsam schuldig sei.*

13. Cf. Ernst Troeltsch, *The Social Teachings of the Christian Churches*, translated by Olive Wyon (New York, 1931), II, 528 ff. A careful account of Luther's and Melanchthon's political ideas may be found in Werner Elert, *Morphologie des Luthertums* (München, 1931–32), II, 291–395.

14. Luther, *op. cit.*

15. As quoted in Cotton Mather, *Magnalia Christi Americana*, Book III, Part II, chap. 1, paragraph 12. Perry Miller, *Orthodoxy in Massachusetts, 1630–1650* (Cambridge, 1933), calls attention in various places to the importance of the turn from criticism to construction; cf. pp. 146 f., 176 f.

CHAPTER II

1. V. L. Parrington, "The Puritan Divines, 1620–1720," in *Cambridge History of American Literature*, I, 32, 41.

2. *Bradford's History of Plymouth Plantation, 1606–1646*, edited by William T. Davis (New York, 1908), pp. 44–46.

3. "Winthrop's Conclusions for the Plantation in New England," in Massachusetts Historical Society's *Proceedings*, 1864–65, pp. 417 ff.

4. John Cotton, *God's Promise to His Plantations* (London, 1630). Reprinted in *Old South Leaflets*, Series XII, No. 6 (Boston, 1894).

5. Roger Williams, *Experiments of Spiritual Life & Health, and their Preservatives In which the weakest Child of God may get Assurance of his Spiritual Life and Blessedness And the Strongest may finde proportionable Discoveries of his Christian Growth, and the means of it* (Lon-

don, 1652, reprinted in partial facsimile, Providence, 1862), pp. 48 f., 56.

6. *The Letters of Roger Williams*, edited by John Russell Bartlett. Publications of the Narragansett Club, First Series, Vol. VI (Providence, 1874), p. 168.

7. Robert Barclay, *An Apology for the True Christian Divinity*, Fourth Proposition (Philadelphia, 1908), p. 15.

8. Isaac Pennington, *Works* (4th ed., Philadelphia, 1863), II, 371.

9. Peter Bayne, "English Puritanism: Its Character and History," an introduction to *Documents Relating to the Settlement of the Church of England by the Act of Uniformity of 1662* (London, 1862), p. 16.

10. Williston Walker, *The Creeds and Platforms of Congregationalism* (New York, 1893), p. 370.

11. Richard Baxter, *A Holy Commonwealth, or Political Aphorisms* (London, 1659), theses 24, 26, 28 (pp. 18, 42, 43).

12. As quoted in William C. Braithwaite, *The Beginnings of Quakerism* (London, 1912), p. 97.

13. *The Works of George Fox* (Philadelphia and New York, 1831), I, 96; cf. p. 108.

14. Pennington, *Works*, II, 98, 96; cf. I, 79 ff.

15. Roger Williams, *The Bloudy Tenent of Persecution for Cause of Conscience Discussed*, edited for the Hanserd Knollys Society by Edward Bean Underhill (London, 1848), p. 8.

16. As quoted by Robert Barclay, *Inner Life of the Religious Societies of the Commonwealth* (London, 1879), pp. 306 f.

17. In his preface to the *Survey of the Summe of Church Discipline* (London, 1648), Thomas Hooker wrote: "The Summe is, we doubt not what we practise, but its beyond all doubt, that all men are liars, and we are in the number of those poor feeble men, either we do, or may erre, though we do not know it, what we have learned we do professe, and yet professe still to live, that we may learn." This spirit seems at least as characteristic of the Puritan leaders as the pretension to infallibility which their critics find in them.

18. Robert Barclay, *Apology*, Second and Third Propositions, pp. 13, 15.

19. *Of the Laws of Ecclesiastical Polity*, Book II, introduction and chap. 1.

20. Samuel E. Morison, *The American Pronaos* (New York, 1936), pp. 15 ff.

21. From the second of the "Rules and Precepts that are observed in the Colledge" as given in *New England's First Fruits*, Massachusetts Historical Society, *Collections*, Vol. I (2d ed., Boston, 1806), p. 243.

22. John Eliot, *The Christian Commonwealth: or, The Civil Policy of the Rising Kingdom of Jesus Christ*, Massachusetts Historical Society, *Collections*, Series III, Vol. IX (Boston, 1846), p. 134. Cf. F. J. Powicke, *Some Unpublished Correspondence of the Reverend Richard Baxter and the Reverend John Eliot, the Apostle to the American Indians, 1656–1682* (Manchester, 1931).

23. Williams, *op. cit.*, pp. 272 ff.; cf. pp. 2, 87.

24. An example of the constitutional use of the Scriptures may be found in John Cotton's much quoted *Abstract of the Laws of New England*, reprinted in Peter Force, *Tracts and Other Papers, Relating Principally to the Origin, Settlement, and Progress of the Colonies in North America* (Washington, 1844), Vol. III. Cotton's work represents, for the most part, no more than an attempt to codify the existing laws of church and state, while the scriptural references which accompany the text give assurance that the laws are in accordance with the constitution rather than deduced or copied from it. Cf. I. M. Calder, *The New Haven Colony* (New Haven, 1934), pp. 42 ff. It is possible of course to interpret the significance of biblical constitutionalism in purely negative terms. Since the Bible contains so many different books and views it may be claimed that it offered opportunity for every sort of interpretation and that its primary use was as a weapon against traditional forms or as an instrument of criticism rather than of construction. Cf. T. C. Hall, *The Religious Background of American Culture*, pp. 22, 25, 53, 55, and H. W. Schneider, *The Puritan Mind* (New York, 1930), pp. 52–53. To make this claim is to forget that despite all its diversity the Bible has a certain unity — that not only of the Hebraic but also of the prophetic outlook on life. If its diversity fostered freedom, its unity gave direction to that freedom.

25. *Letters of Roger Williams*, p. 212.

26. Pennington, *Works*, IV, 263 ff.; III, 45, 55, 244; Barclay, *Apology*, pp. 137 ff.

27. Rufus Jones, *The Later Periods of Quakerism* (London, 1921), I, 457. Cf. Braithwaite, *The Beginnings of Quakerism*, pp. 289 f., 300, 390.

28. Perry Miller, *op. cit.*, p. 47.

29. Gerhard Gloege, *Reich Gottes und Kirche im Neuen Testament* (Gütersloh, 1929), pp. 201 ff.

30. Benz, *Ecclesia Spiritualis*, pp. 134 ff.

31. As quoted in Hutchinson, *History of the Colony of Massachusetts Bay* (2d ed., London, 1770), I, 497.

32. H. D. Foster, "Calvin's Program for a Puritan State in Geneva, 1536–1541," *Harvard Theological Review*, I, 402 ff.

33. John Cotton, *Of the Holinesse of Church Members* (London, 1650), pp. 32, 43 f. Cf. Perry Miller, *op. cit.*, pp. 196 f.

34. The Savoy Declaration, Part I, chap. 26, sec. ii, in Walker, *Creeds and Platforms*, pp. 395 f. Cf. John Cotton, *The Way of the Congregational Churches Cleared* (London, 1648), Part II, pp. 5 f.

35. Isaac Sharpless, *A Quaker Experiment in Government* (Philadelphia, 1898); Rufus Jones, *The Quakers in the American Colonies* (London, 1923), pp. xiv, xx, 171 ff., 475 ff., *et passim*.

36. John Cotton, *An Exposition of the thirteenth Chapter of the Revelation* (London, 1656), p. 72. Cf. his *A Briefe Exposition with Practicall observations upon the Whole Book of Ecclesiastes* (London, 1654), especially pp. 164–68.

37. As quoted in Williams, *The Bloudy Tenent*, pp. 219 f.

38. Hooker's sermon of May 31, 1638, in Connecticut Historical Society, *Collections*, Vol. I (Hartford, 1860), p. 20.

39. As quoted in Williams, *The Bloudy Tenent*, p. 219.

40. As quoted in Perry Miller, *op. cit.*, p. 246.

41. *Winthrop's Journal " History of New England,"* edited by James Kendall Hosmer (New York, 1908), II, 238 f.

42. *The Bloudy Tenent*, pp. 211 f.

43. James Bryce, *The American Commonwealth* (Chicago, 1891), I, 299 f.

44. Henry Adams, *History of the United States during the Administration of Thomas Jefferson* (popular edition, New York, 1930), Book I, p. 116.

45. John Cotton, *The Keyes of the Kingdom of Heaven* (Boston, 1843), p. 3.

46. Cf. Hooker's Preface to the *Survey of the Summe of Church Discipline*.

47. *An Exposition of the thirteenth Chapter of the Revelation*, p. 17.

48. *The Keyes of the Kingdom*, p. 22.

49. *The Bloudy Tenent*, p. 61.

50. *An Exposition of the thirteenth Chapter of the Revelation*, pp. 30 f., 121.

51. William Ames, *Conscience With the Power and Cases Thereof* (London, 1643), pp. 2, 4.

52. Pennington, *Works*, II, 234; I, 443; Barclay, *op. cit.*, pp. 461 f.

53. R. H. Tawney, *Religion and the Rise of Capitalism* (New York, Harcourt, Brace, 1926), p. 127.

54. Isabel Grubb, *Quakerism and Industry Before 1800* (London, 1929), especially chaps. 2 and 6.

CHAPTER III

1. A. E. Taylor, *The Faith of a Moralist* (New York, 1930), II, 1–3. Cf. Benz, *Ecclesia Spiritualis*, p. 2.
2. Jeremiah 31:31–34.
3. *Op. cit.*, pp. iv, viii.
4. *The Works of George Fox*, I, 90.
5. Pennington, *Works*, II, 380 f.; Braithwaite, *The Second Period of Quakerism* (London, 1919), p. 451.
6. C. F. Adams, ed., *Antinomianism in the Colony of Massachusetts Bay, 1636–1638, including the Short Story and Other Documents* (Boston, 1894), pp. 95 ff.
7. Cf. John Cotton, *The Covenant of Gods free Grace* (London, 1645), pp. 27 ff.; *The Covenant of Grace* (London, 1655), pp. 124 ff.; *Christ the Fountaine of Life* (London, 1651), especially pp. 67 ff.; *The Way of Life* (London, 1641), especially the fourth treatise in this volume, "The Life of Faith," pp. 255 ff. Cf. also K. E. Murdock, "The Puritans and the New Testament," in Colonial Society of Massachusetts, *Publications*, XXV, 239 ff.
8. *Exposition of the thirteenth Chapter of the Revelation*, pp. 173 f., 106 f., 154.
9. As quoted in S. E. Morison, *Builders of the Bay Colony* (Boston, 1930), p. 128.
10. As quoted in Murdock, *op. cit.*
11. Savoy Declaration and Westminster Confession. Cf. Walker, *op. cit.*, pp. 377 f.
12. *Survey of the Summe of Church Discipline*, preface.
13. *The Keyes of the Kingdom*, p. 2.
14. As quoted in Parrington, *op. cit.*, I, 143, 144.
15. Jonathan Edwards, *The Works of President Edwards* (10 vols., New York, 1829), I, 60, 61; cf. V, 501; III, 103 f.; VI, 293 ff.
16. G. C. Cell, *The Rediscovery of John Wesley* (New York, 1935). Cf. Umphrey Lee, *John Wesley and Modern Religion* (Nashville, 1936), pp. 126 ff. The question whether Wesley was genuinely Arminian or a Calvinist can be debated interminably, not only because he was not a wholly consistent theologian but also because such terms as Arminian and Calvinist are ambiguous. If Calvinism means the static, institutionalized creed of determinism Wesley was certainly no Calvinist—but neither was John Calvin. Static faith changes the meaning of all the terms which dynamic faith uses to express its trust in the living God, its awareness of the infinite dependence of man and the world upon

him. Against that static Calvinism Wesley reacted strongly. But he did preach and believe in the divine initiative to which man was bound to respond. His religion was theocentric and much more like that of seventeenth century English Calvinists than like that of eighteenth century Arminians. On the contrast of dynamic and static see below, chap. 5.

17. Finney, the lawyer turned evangelist and living in a time when institutionalized conceptions prevailed, thought of sovereignty in terms of "moral government." The rule of God according to his definition was one of law more than of living, personal will. Yet the Edwardean influence is unmistakable in his writings. See his *Lectures on Systematic Theology, embracing Lectures on Moral Government,* etc. (Oberlin, 1846), especially Lectures I–IV.

18. *The Journal and Essays of John Woolman,* edited by Amelia Mott Gummere (Rancocas edition, New York, 1922), p. 156.

19. Cf. Edwards, *Works,* VII, 317 f.

20. *Ibid.,* II, 18 ff.

21. Jonathan Edwards, *Christian Love as Manifested in Heart and Life* (6th ed., Philadelphia), p. 87; cf. *Works,* VII, 459 f.

22. *Works,* IV, 46 f.

23. Archibald Alexander, *Thoughts on Religious Experience* (3d ed., Philadelphia), pp. 84 f.

24. Finney, *op. cit.,* p. 498.

25. Cf. Umphrey Lee, *op. cit.,* pp. 131 f.; Cell, *op. cit.,* chaps. 3–5. Note also Edwards' use of the Scriptures in his treatises on original sin and in "The End for which God Created the World."

26. Cf. Edwards, "The Distinguishing Marks of a Work of the Spirit of God," *Works,* III, 559 ff., and "A Treatise Concerning Religious Affections," V, 1 ff.

27. *Works,* V, 13; cf. VI, 185 f., 238 ff.

28. *Ibid.,* V, 151.

29. *Ibid.,* V, 10 ff.

30. Cell, *op. cit.,* p. 128 f. Cf. Edwards, *Works,* V, 249 ff.

31. *Christian Love,* pp. 337 f.

32. *Ibid.,* pp. 249 f.; cf. *Works,* III, 118 ff.

33. *Works,* I, 61.

34. Woolman's *Journal,* p. 156 f.

35. John Wesley, *Sermons on Several Occasions* (New York, 1815), I, 461 ff., 468.

36. Edwards, *Works,* IV, 296.

37. From Whitefield's sermon, "The Lord is Our Light," in John Gillies, *Memoirs of George Whitefield* (New Haven, 1834), p. 588.

38. J. O. Choules and Thomas Smith, *The Origin and History of Missions* (4th ed., Boston, 1837), II, 234 ff.; Kenneth Scott Latourette, *A History of Christian Missions in China* (New York, 1932), pp. 205 ff.

39. G. H. Barnes, *The Anti-Slavery Impulse, 1830–1844* (New York, 1933), pp. 161 ff.

40. Emerson Davis, *The Half-Century; or a History of Changes That Have Taken Place and Events That Have Transpired, Chiefly in the United States Between 1800 and 1850* (Boston, 1851); Barnes, *op. cit.*, pp. 17 ff.; J. T. Adams, *Provincial Society* (New York, 1927), p. 284; C. R. Fish, *The Rise of the Common Man* (New York, 1929), pp. 179 ff., 256 ff.

41. Cf. J. T. Adams, *Revolutionary New England* (Boston, 1923), pp. 177–78; W. M. Gewehr, *The Great Awakening in Virginia, 1740–1790* (Durham, N. C., 1930), pp. 187 ff.; E. R. Taylor, *Methodism and Politics* (Cambridge, 1935).

42. G. Adolf Koch, *Republican Religion. The American Revolution and the Cult of Reason* (New York, 1933).

43. Cf. R. W. Chambers, *Thomas More* (New York, 1935), p. 390.

CHAPTER IV

1. II Esdras 4:34.

2. Massachusetts Historical Society, *Collections*, Series III, Vol. IX, pp. 129, 133.

3. *The Survey of the Summe of Church Discipline*, preface.

4. James K. Hosmer, *The Life of Young Sir Henry Vane* (Boston and New York, 1888), pp. 428 ff.

5. *The Works of George Fox*, I, 120 f.

6. *Ibid.*, II, 88.

7. As quoted in Braithwaite, *The Beginnings of Quakerism*, p. 401.

8. Sharpless, *A Quaker Experiment in Government*, pp. 28 f., 41, 103, 112 f., 152 f., *et passim*; Rufus Jones, *The Quakers in the American Colonies*, pp. 175 ff., 184 f., 478 ff.

9. *Works*, I, 69.

10. Cf. C. G. Finney, *Memoirs* (New York, 1876), pp. 9, 13.

11. Cf. also George Santayana, *Obiter Scripta* (New York, 1936), pp. 284 ff.

12. *Works*, VII, 170; cf. p. 168.

13. *Journal*, p. 308 f.

14. Samuel Hopkins, "A Treatise on the Millenium," in *Works* (Boston, 1854), II, 226.

15. Edwards, *Works*, IV, 128.

16. *Ibid.*, IV, 120 f.

17. *Ibid.*, III, 325.

18. *Ibid.*, III, 409 ff., 413 ff.

19. William Ellery Channing, *Works* (one-volume ed., Boston, 1888), pp. 427 f.

20. Hopkins, *Works*, II, 265, 261 ff.

21. Edwards, *Works*, III, 404–9.

22. Hopkins, *Works*, II, 271–87.

23. Wesley, *Sermons*, II, 14, 15, 18.

24. Wesley, *Letters* (Standard ed., London, 1931), VIII, 67.

25. *The Journal and Essays of John Woolman*, pp. 334 ff.

26. A somewhat similar development in the Franciscan-Dominican movement is described by Benz, *op. cit.*, pp. 175 ff.

27. Cf. Edwards' sermon, "Pressing into the Kingdom," *Works*, V, 453 ff.

28. Cf. above, chap. 3, n. 41.

29. Hopkins, *Works*, I, 116 f., II, 551 ff., 587.

30. Fish, *Rise of the Common Man*, chap. 12.

31. Clara E. Sears, *Days of Delusion* (New York, 1924).

32. *Practical Sermons* (New York, 1858); cf. "The Better Country," "On Heaven," "Holiness Alone Fits for Heaven."

33. Lyman Beecher, *Works* (Boston, 1852), II, 441.

34. On the relation of Channing and Transcendentalism to the religious Awakening and revivals see below, chap. 5, ii.

35. W. H. Channing, *A Memoir of William Ellery Channing* (9th ed., Boston, 1868), I, 63; cf. II, 159, 255.

36. Cf. "The Great Purpose of Christianity," *Works*, 246 ff.; "Immortality," 354 f.; "The Perfect Life," 931 ff., especially 1006 f.; "The Future Life," 359 ff.

37. *Works*, p. 920; cf. also the discourses on war and slavery and "The Philanthropist."

38. James Gray, *A Sketch of the Present Conditions and Prospects of the Christian Church* (Baltimore, 1821); Lyman Beecher, *Works*, II, 441.

39. Cf. Hopkins' introduction to Emerson Davis, *The Half-Century*, pp. xvi ff.

40. Stephen Colwell, *New Themes for the Protestant Clergy* (New York, 1851).

41. *The Millenial Harbinger* (Bethany, Va., 1830), I, 1, 5.

42. *Ibid.*, p. 34.

43. *Lectures on Systematic Theology*, p. 496.

44. *Ibid.*, pp. 550–53.

45. Gilbert H. Barnes and Dwight L. Dumond, *Letters of Theodore Dwight Weld, Angelina Grimké Weld and Sarah Grimké* (New York, 1934), I, 297 f.

46. Edward Beecher, "The Scriptural Philosophy of Congregationalism and of Councils," in *Bibliotheca Sacra*, XXII (1865), 312.

47. Barnes, *Letters of T. D. Weld*, I, 243.

48. *Ibid.*, I, 318 ff.

49. Hopkins, *Works*, II, 586 ff.

50. Barnes, *Letters of T. D. Weld*, I, 247 f.

51. Parrington, *op. cit.*, III, 23.

52. Samuel Harris, *The Kingdom of Christ on Earth* (Andover, 1874), pp. 65, 253, 255.

53. Washington Gladden, *Burning Questions* (New York, 1890), pp. 243 ff.

54. I am especially indebted for information on this point to an unpublished ms. by Dr. Vernon P. Bodein of Hartford, Conn.

Chapter V

1. Bergson, *The Two Sources of Morality and Religion*, p. 227.

2. F. H. Foster, *A Genetic History of New England Theology* (Chicago, 1907), pp. 31 f.

3. Parrington, *op. cit.*, I, 107.

4. "The Bostonian Ebenezer," published as an appendix to Book I of *Magnalia Christi Americana*.

5. *Bonifacius: An Essay upon the Good that is to be devised and designed by those who desire to answer the great end of life*, etc. (Boston, 1710). Later published in many editions under the title *Essays To Do Good*.

6. Parrington, *op. cit.*, I, 125 ff.

7. Lyman Beecher, *Works*, I, 287 f.

8. Cf. Beecher's sermons, "The Bible a Code of Laws," *Works*, II, 154 ff., and "The Government of God Desirable," II, 5 ff.

9. *Works*, I, 189 f.

10. *Ibid.*, I, 322.

11. *Ibid.*, II, 219.

12. *Ibid.*, I, 332 f.

13. *Ibid.*, II, 106, 110 f. On the mind of New England in this period cf. Henry Adams, *History of the United States in the Administration of Thomas Jefferson*, Book I, chap. 3.

14. Beecher, *Works*, II, 222, 223, 228.

15. Leonard Woolsey Bacon, *A History of American Christianity* (New York, 1897), chaps. 11 and 12, p. 175.

16. R. E. Thompson, *A History of the Presbyterian Churches in the United States* (New York, 1895), pp. 95 ff.; W. W. Sweet, *Methodism in American History* (New York, 1933), pp. 332 ff., also pp. 272, 309, 325, 332; Rufus Jones, *The Later Periods of Quakerism* (London, 1921), I, 435 ff., 488 ff.; Bacon, *op. cit.*, 292 ff.

17. Typical expressions of this spirit may be found in Lyman Beecher, *Works*, I, 324 ff.; Horace Bushnell, *The Crisis of the Church* (Hartford, 1835), and *An Oration . . . on the Principles of National Greatness* (New Haven, 1837); Henry C. Fish, " The Earth Tributary to Christ's Kingdom," *National Preacher*, Ser. III, Vol. IV, no. 11 (Nov., 1865) and other sermons in that collection; Josiah Strong, *The New Era, or the Coming Kingdom* (New York, 1893), and *Expansion Under New World Conditions* (New York, 1900).

18. Cf. Nathaniel Hawthorne, " The Celestial Railroad," in *Mosses from an Old Manse.*

19. Calvin Colton, *History and Character of American Revivals of Religion* (2d ed., London, 1832), pp. 2–7.

20. Bushnell, *The Crisis of the Church*, pp. 9, 10, 14.

21. *Memoir*, I, 127.

22. *Works*, p. 7.

23. " The New England Reformers," in *Essays, Second Series.*

24. Nicolas Berdyaev, *The Meaning of History* (New York, 1936); Carl Becker, *The Heavenly City of the Eighteenth Century Philosophers* (New Haven, 1932); Edwyn Bevan, *The Hope of the World To Come Underlying Judaism and Christianity* (London, 1930).

25. W. A. Hinds, *American Communities and Co-operative Colonies* (3d ed., Chicago, 1908); Charles Nordhoff, *Communistic Societies of the United States* (New York, 1875); J. J. Sessler, *Communal Pietism Among Early American Moravians* (New York, 1933); James Dombrowski, *The Early Days of Christian Socialism in America* (New York, 1936).

26. *Religion in the Making* (New York, 1926), p. 16.

27. *Christian Nurture* (New York, 1862), pp. 22 f.; *Sermons on Living Subjects* (New York, 1872), pp. 138 ff.

28. Cf. *God in Christ, Vicarious Sacrifice, Forgiveness and Law.*

29. This is particularly true of the *Theology for a Social Gospel* (New York, 1918).

INDEX

Revised January, 1970

hARPER ⚜ TORChBOOKS

† The New American Nation Series, edited by Henry Steele Commager and Richard B. Morris.
‡ American Perspectives series, edited by Bernard Wishy and William E. Leuchtenburg.
α History of Europe series, edited by J. H. Plumb.
§ The Library of Religion and Culture, edited by Benjamin Nelson.
‖ Researches in the Social, Cultural, and Behavioral Sciences, edited by Benjamin Nelson.
Σ Harper Modern Science Series, edited by James R. Newman.
° Not for sale in Canada.
+ Documentary History of the United States series, edited by Richard B. Morris.
# Documentary History of Western Civilization series, edited by Eugene C. Black and Leonard W. Levy.
A The Economic History of the United States series, edited by Henry David et al.
¶ European Perspectives series, edited by Eugene C. Black.
** Contemporary Essays series, edited by Leonard W Levy.
* The Stratum Series, edited by John Hale.

History: Renaissance & Reformation

JACOB BURCKHARDT: The Civilization of the Renaissance in Italy. *Introduction by Benjamin Nelson and Charles Trinkaus. Illus.* Vol. I TB/40; Vol. II TB/41

JOEL HURSTFIELD: The Elizabethan Nation TB/1312

ALFRED VON MARTIN: Sociology of the Renaissance. ° *Introduction by W. K. Ferguson* TB/1099

J. H. PARRY: The Establishment of the European Hegemony: 1415-1715: *Trade and Exploration in the Age of the Renaissance* TB/1045

History: Modern European

MAX BELOFF: The Age of Absolutism, 1660-1815 TB/1062

ALAN BULLOCK: Hitler, A Study in Tyranny. ° *Revised Edition. Illus.* TB/1123

JOHANN GOTTLIEB FICHTE: Addresses to the German Nation. *Ed. with Intro. by George A. Kelly* ¶ TB/1366

H. STUART HUGHES: The Obstructed Path: *French Social Thought in the Years of Desperation* TB/1451

JOHAN HUIZINGA: Dutch Cviilization in the 17th Century and Other Essays TB/1453

JOHN MCMANNERS: European History, 1789-1914: *Men, Machines and Freedom* TB/1419

FRANZ NEUMANN: Behemoth: *The Structure and Practice of National Socialism, 1933-1944* TB/1289

A. J. P. TAYLOR: From Napoleon to Lenin: *Historical Essays* ° TB/1268

H. R. TREVOR-ROPER: Historical Essays TB/1269

Philosophy

HENRI BERGSON: Time and Free Will: *An Essay on the Immediate Data of Consciousness* ° TB/1021

G. W. F. HEGEL: Phenomenology of Mind. ° ‖ *Introduction by George Lichtheim* TB/1303

H. J. PATON: The Categorical Imperative: *A Study in Kant's Moral Philosophy* TB/1325

MICHAEL POLANYI: Personal Knowledge: *Towards a Post-Critical Philosophy* TB/1158

LUDWIG WITTGENSTEIN: The Blue and Brown Books ° TB/1211

LUDWIG WITTGENSTEIN: Notebooks, 1914-1916 TB/1441

Political Science & Government

C. E. BLACK: The Dynamics of Modernization: *A Study in Comparative History* TB/1321

DENIS W. BROGAN: Politics in America. *New Introduction by the Author* TB/1469

KARL R. POPPER: The Open Society and Its Enemies *Vol. I: The Spell of Plato* TB/1101 *Vol: II: The High Tide of Prophecy: Hegel, Marx, and the Aftermath* TB/1102

CHARLES SCHOTTLAND, Ed.: The Welfare State ** TB/1323

JOSEPH A. SCHUMPETER: Capitalism, Socialism and Democracy TB/3008

PETER WOLL, Ed.: Public Administration and Policy: *Selected Essays* TB/1284

Psychology

LUDWIG BINSWANGER: Being-in-the-World: *Selected Papers.* ‖ *Trans. with Intro. by Jacob Needleman* TB/1365

MIRCEA ELIADE: Cosmos and History: *The Myth of the Eternal Return* § TB/2050

SIGMUND FREUD: On Creativity and the Unconscious: *Papers on the Psychology of Art, Literature, Love, Religion.* § *Intro. by Benjamin Nelson* TB/45

J. GLENN GRAY: The Warriors: *Reflections on Men in Battle. Introduction by Hannah Arendt* TB/1294

WILLIAM JAMES: Psychology: *The Briefer Course. Edited with an Intro. by Gordon Allport* TB/1034

Religion

TOR ANDRAE: Mohammed: *The Man and his Faith* TB/62

KARL BARTH: Church Dogmatics: *A Selection. Intro. by H. Hollwitzer. Ed. by G. W. Bromiley* TB/95

NICOLAS BERDYAEV: The Destiny of Man TB/61

MARTIN BUBER: The Prophetic Faith TB/73

MARTIN BUBER: Two Types of Faith: *Interpenetration of Judaism and Christianity* TB/75

RUDOLF BULTMANN: History and Eschatology: *The Presence of Eternity* TB/91

EDWARD CONZE: Buddhism: *Its Essence and Development. Foreword by Arthur Waley* TB/58

H. G. CREEL: Confucius and the Chinese Way TB/63

FRANKLIN EDGERTON, Trans. & Ed.: The Bhagavad Gita TB/115

M. S. ENSLIN: Christian Beginnings TB/5

M. S. ENSLIN: The Literature of the Christian Movement TB/6

HENRI FRANKFORT: Ancient Egyptian Religion: *An Interpretation* TB/77

IMMANUEL KANT: Religion Within the Limits of Reason Alone. *Introduction by Theodore M. Greene and John Silber* TB/67

GABRIEL MARCEL: Homo Viator: *Introduction to a Metaphysic of Hope* TB/397

H. RICHARD NIEBUHR: Christ and Culture TB/3

H. RICHARD NIEBUHR: The Kingdom of God in America TB/49

SWAMI NIKHILANANDA, Trans. & Ed.: The Upanishads TB/114

F. SCHLEIERMACHER: The Christian Faith. *Introduction by Richard R. Niebuhr.* Vol. I TB/108 Vol. II TB/109

Sociology and Anthropology

KENNETH B. CLARK: Dark Ghetto: *Dilemmas of Social Power. Foreword by Gunnar Myrdal* TB/1317

KENNETH CLARK & JEANNETTE HOPKINS: A Relevant War Against Poverty: *A Study of Community Action Programs and Observable Social Change* TB/1480

GARY T. MARX: Protest and Prejudice: *A Study of Belief in the Black Community* TB/1435

ROBERT K. MERTON, LEONARD BROOM, LEONARD S. COTTRELL, JR., Editors: Sociology Today: *Problems and Prospects* ‖ Vol. I TB/1173; Vol. II TB/1174

GILBERT OSOFSKY: Harlem: The Making of a Ghetto: *Negro New York, 1890-1930* TB/1381

PHILIP RIEFF: The Triumph of the Therapeutic: *Uses of Faith After Freud* TB/1360

GEORGE ROSEN: Madness in Society: *Chapters in the Historical Sociology of Mental Illness.* ‖ *Preface by Benjamin Nelson* TB/1337